PENNSYLVANIA
YESTERDAY & TODAY

BLAIR SEITZ

Voyageur Press

Library of Congress Cataloging-in-Publication Data

Seitz, Blair.
  Pennsylvania yesterday & today / by Blair Seitz.
      p. cm.
  Includes index.
  ISBN-13: 978-0-7603-2830-9 (hardbound)
  1. Pennsylvania—Pictorial works. 2. Pennsylvania—History—Pictorial works. 3. Pennsylvania—History, Local—Pictorial works. 4. Historic buildings—Pennsylvania—Pictorial works. 5. Historic sites—Pennsylvania—Pictorial works. I. Title. II. Title: Pennsylvania yesterday and today.
F150.S445 2007
974.80022′2—dc22
                                    2007011530

Editor: Josh Leventhal
Designer: Julie Vermeer, Melissa Khaira

Printed in China

On the front cover: (top) Benjamin Franklin Parkway, Philadelphia, yesterday and today. *(bottom)* Amish couple ride in buggy, Lancaster County.
On the back cover: (top) Pittsburgh skyline, yesterday and today. *(right)* Independence Hall, Philadelphia, yesterday and today.
On the title page: State Street and State Capitol Building, Harrisburg, 2007. *(inset)* Postcard view of State Capitol, Harrisburg.

Contents

ACKNOWLEDGMENTS

I would like to thank the following individuals and organizations for their help in the creation of this book: Georg Sheets, author and historian, for his assistance with locating and providing some of the historic photographs; the Pennsylvania Historical and Museum Commission State Archives, for providing many of the historical photographs printed in this book, with particular thanks to the staff for their many hours of patient assistance while researching the photographs; the York County Heritage Trust, for providing several photographs of the City of York; and the Historical Society of Western Pennsylvania Library and Archives, for providing some of the historic photographs of Pittsburgh.

ILLUSTRATIONS CREDITS

Unless otherwise noted, all color photography is by the author. Archival material is from the Voyageur Press collection, unless otherwise noted.

Library and Archives Division, Historical Society of Western Pennsylvania, Pittsburgh: pp. 131 top and bottom right, 132, 137 bottom left, 138 bottom, 139 top, 140 top

Library of Congress, Prints & Photographs Division: pp. 7, 12 top, 14 top left, 15 bottom, 18 top, 22 bottom, 25 bottom, 26 top left and top right, 30 left, 34 both, 40, 42 top right, 44 all, 46 bottom right, 54 top, 56, 57 top left, 58 bottom right, 60 all, 62 top, 64 right, 72 top, 74 top, 77 top left, 82–83 top, 84 bottom, 86 top, 87 top right, 90 top, 92–93 bottom, 100 top, 102 middle left, 102 bottom, 113 top, 114–115 top, 116 bottom, 117 top left, 118 all, 128–129 top, 128 bottom, 130 top, 133 bottom right, 137 top left, 140 bottom

Pennsylvania State Archives: pp. 3, 8 bottom, 10 left, 12 bottom, 14 top right, 16, 18 bottom left and bottom right, 20 top, 23 bottom, 24 bottom left, 26 bottom left and bottom right, 30 right, 32 both, 37 bottom left, 38 top left and top right, 42 bottom, 46 top, 48 top, 49 top, 50, 51 bottom left, 52, 54 bottom, 58 bottom left and top right, 64 left, 66 both, 70 top left and bottom left, 71 top, 72 bottom, 73 top right, 74 bottom, 76 left, 78 bottom, 79 top left, 80 bottom, 81 top left, 82 middle, 86 bottom, 88 both, 91 top left and bottom left, 93 top left, 94 both, 96 both, 100 bottom left, 104 top left and bottom left, 106 all, 108 top left and top right, 109 top, 110 both, 113 bottom, 120 left, 121 top left, 123 top, 124 both, 126 both, 135 bottom left, 136 top; front cover top right, back cover middle

Print and Picture Collection, The Free Library of Philadelphia: p. 11 bottom left

Temple University Libraries, Urban Archives, Philadelphia: p. 11 top left

York County Heritage Trust: p. 84 top

Pennsylvania Art Project, WPA promotional poster, late 1930s

Above: Penn's Treaty with the Indians, *by Edwin A. Abbey, State Capitol Building, Harrisburg*

Right: *Cornplanter Tract, Warren, 1940*

World's End Native American Annual Powwow, Sullivan County

NATIVE AMERICANS

The earliest residents of what is now the Commonwealth of Pennsylvania were the native tribes that settled within the area's rich landscapes of dense forest, lush valleys, and flowing waterways. The Lenni Lenape, Susquehannock, Erie, Iroquois, and other tribes first encountered European explorers in the early 1600s, when Swedish, Finnish, and then Dutch settlers began to trade with the locals. As more Europeans arrived, with their diseases and their firepower, the Native Americans had little means of resistance, and their numbers dwindled dramatically.

In 1682, William Penn arrived to take over the land grant bestowed to him by King Charles II of England. Penn befriended the local Native Americans and purchased additional land rights from them. He assured the tribal leaders that he and his followers "came not to injure others, but to do good." While the peace that Penn fostered would eventually be betrayed by his descendents, Penn's government maintained a friendly relationship with the native tribes for some years.

Honoring Penn's diplomatic efforts, Edwin A. Abbey's painting *Penn's Treaty with the Indians* is one of several large murals adorning the House Chamber of the State Capitol in Harrisburg.

The Cornplanter Tract, in northwestern Pennsylvania's Warren County, was the last surviving Native American community in the state. The land was granted to Cornplanter, a chief of the Seneca Nation, in 1791, in appreciation for his diplomatic efforts among the native tribes of Pennsylvania and Ohio. The tract passed on to Cornplanter's heirs, who remained on the land until 1964. After the Kinzua Dam was completed in 1965, the former Seneca lands were flooded and became submerged within the Allegheny Reservoir.

Today, the offspring of Pennsylvania's native tribes gather at various locations throughout the state in celebrations incorporating traditional dance, drumming, and other sacred rites. The Kipona Powwow draws Native Americans to Harrisburg's City Island, on the Susquehanna River, each September, and the annual Eastern Delaware Nations Powwow is held at the county fairgrounds in Forksville, among several other events.

NEW SWEDEN

More than forty years before the arrival of William Penn, the New Sweden Company established the first European settlement along the Delaware River in 1638. The company made several expeditions to the New World to trade with the Lenape Indians, and Sweden retained control of the colony until 1655, when it was annexed by the Dutch New Netherlands. Today, the Morton Homestead affirms the place of Swedes and Finns among America's earliest European settlers.

The historic reconstruction of a near-fallen shack, initially called the John Morton House, in Delaware County has left historians debating the home's origins. The destruction and subsequent rebuilding of the house in the 1930s resulted in the loss of many details in the foundation, framework, and window treatment that would allow researchers to confidently identify it as the home of Swede John Morton. The house was renamed the Morton Homestead by the Pennsylvania Historical and Museum Commission after it acquired the property. Some historians suggest that the home be renamed as Morton Mortonson's house, or simply as a ferry house. Morton, the head of the Mortonson (also spelled Mortensen or Mortenson, and later shortened to Morton) household, was an early settler of New Sweden, although little is known about the first members who arrived here. It is likely that

Window and wooden pail, Morton Homestead

Morton volunteered for adventure, since the Swedes did not intend to colonize and remain in the New World. Many early Swedish settlers were war deserters, opting for life in the foreign wilderness in lieu of imprisonment.

Morton Homestead, 1930s

ELFRETH'S ALLEY, PHILADELPHIA

Elfreth's Alley, Fete Day, 1969

The oldest continuously occupied residential street in the United States is located in the heart of Philadelphia's Old City. The alley was created in about 1702, and Jeremiah Elfreth built the first homes here in the 1720s. The earliest occupants of Elfreth's Alley were mostly artisans and tradesmen, but through the years, the residents of this narrow street have come from all walks of life. Many immigrant and working-class families came to live on the cobblestone street during Philadelphia's industrial boom in the late nineteenth and early twentieth centuries.

In 1934, the Elfreth's Alley Association was formed to preserve and celebrate this piece of American history, and in 1958, the street became a National Historic Landmark. The residences are still privately owned, but visitors have a chance to tour many of the historic Georgian- and Federal-style homes during Fete Day, held each June since 1934. While the street is often crammed with tourists and re-enactors in period dress during the annual celebration, Elfreth's Alley remains a quiet and charming residential lane.

Elfreth's Alley, 1910

Elfreth's Alley

Above: *Philadelphia aerial and Schuylkill River, 1893*
Right: *Philadelphia aerial, with Customs House, 1930s*

Philadelphia aerial, and Delaware River, from the East

PHILADELPHIA

Philadelphia was a planned city conceived by William Penn to foster the principles of religious and political freedom and to encourage economic prosperity. Penn envisioned a city of open spaces, wide streets, and public parks—"a greene Country Towne, which will never be burnt, and always be wholesome." While the "City of Brotherly Love" reflected some of Penn's ideals, Philadelphia spread rapidly beyond its original borders, absorbing many neighboring communities. The grid layout of the streets became interspersed with many narrow alleys cut through the large city blocks. Philadelphia's population increased from about five thousand in 1700 to more than forty-one thousand in 1800. By 1900, the city had 1.3 million residents. Today, with nearly 1.5 million residents, Philadelphia is the fifth-largest city in the United States.

The city is bordered to the east and south by the Delaware River, which forms the boundary between New Jersey and Pennsylvania. The Schuylkill River flows through the city to the west and separates downtown from West Philly. From the 1893 bird's-eye view of the city, and the 1930s-era photo showing the Customs House prominently in the skyline, Philadelphia has grown to include gleaming office buildings and other skyscrapers.

PHILADELPHIA CITY HALL

The 510-foot-high City Hall building, constructed between 1871 and 1901, was the tallest building in Philadelphia until 1987, when the city lifted an unofficial prohibition against building anything taller than City Hall. Since then, the thirty-seven-foot-tall statue of William "Billy" Penn atop the clock tower has been dwarfed by the modern glass towers of Center City, but the refurbished City Hall remains an architectural jewel of Philadelphia.

City Hall, from Broad Street, 1930s

View from City Hall, looking north on Broad Street, circa 1911

View from City Hall, looking west on Market Street

A designated National Historic Landmark, Philadelphia's City Hall is one of the nation's best examples of French Second Empire architecture, and it is credited as being the largest occupied masonry building in the world. Since its conception in 1860, the building has weathered controversy over graft, bribery, maintenance funds, and campaigns to destroy it. Following a several-year project to restore the giant granite walls and sculptures, City Hall is enjoying renewed appreciation. Tours are given to the tower beneath the Penn statue, which gives a grand view of Philadelphia in all directions. The tower's four clock faces are each twenty-six feet in diameter.

Left: *City Hall, from JFK Plaza*
Below: *City Hall, 1876*

Independence Hall, circa 1776

INDEPENDENCE HALL

On July 4, 1776, representatives from the American colonies convened at the State House of the Province of Pennsylvania in Philadelphia to declare their independence from Great Britain and the "absolute tyranny" of King George III. Standing on a platform above the crowd that had gathered along Walnut Street south of the hall, Colonel John Nixon read "the unanimous declaration of the Thirteen United States of America." Nixon went on to proclaim that a new government would secure the rights of "life, liberty, and the pursuit of happiness." The Declaration of Independence, ratified by the Second Continental Congress, is one of our nation's most significant historical documents.

Eleven years later, in 1787, delegates from the newly independent nation again met in Philadelphia at the newly renamed Independence Hall to draft the Constitution of the United States, establishing the foundation of the new democratic government.

The historic beginnings of the United States of America are relived at Independence Hall, part of Independence National Historical Park. The rooms of the Georgian-style building, completed in 1756, are restored to their late-eighteenth-century appearance and include artifacts from the period.

Independence National Historical Park welcomes millions of visitors every year and encompasses several landmarks of the new nation, including Carpenters' Hall, City Tavern, Congress Hall, the Second Bank of the United States, and other historic buildings. The most recent addition to the complex is the National Constitution Center, opened on Independence Day in 2003. Extensive interactive exhibits present a tour of the key events in the birth of our nation, beginning with the drafting of the Constitution and following through the entry of each state into the Union.

Left: *Independence Hall, July 4, 1993*
Below: *National Constitution Center grand opening, July 4, 2003*

Engraving of Liberty Bell in foundry

Above: *Liberty Bell on tour, 1905*
Right: *Liberty Bell, Independence Hall Declaration Chamber*

THE LIBERTY BELL

An international symbol of freedom, the Liberty Bell was sounded famously in July 1776 to summon Philadelphians to the State House Square for a reading of the Declaration of Independence. The bell was originally cast in London and was delivered to Philadelphia in 1752. Its celebrated crack formed shortly after the bell arrived, and the bell was recast locally before being hung within the steeple of the State House, later known as Independence Hall. The bell's inscription, taken from a Bible verse, reads, "Proclaim LIBERTY throughout all the Land unto all the inhabitants thereof."

The Liberty Bell has had several homes during its 250 years. In the 1850s, it was moved from the steeple to Independence Hall's Declaration Chamber, where it remained until 1976. Around the turn of the twentieth century, the bell often went on tours to cities around the country for exhibitions and other celebrations. In 1905, the Liberty Bell was on its way to California for a brief exhibition in San Francisco.

In anticipation of the nation's bicentennial celebration in 1976, the bell was moved from the cramped Declaration Chamber to its own modern glass-and-steel Liberty Bell Pavilion in the mall north of Independence Hall. It was relocated again—ever so gently and with great precision—to the new and larger Liberty Bell Center in 2003. The center was built, along with the new Independence Visitor Center and National Constitution Center, as part of extensive renewal efforts on the park's mall.

Liberty Bell Center

BEN FRANKLIN AND HIS LEGACY

Benjamin Franklin—inventor, scholar, mediator, scientist, and statesman—was Philadelphia's most illustrious figure of the colonial era, and perhaps of all time. Born in Boston, Franklin moved to Philadelphia in 1723 at the age of seventeen, and the city remained his primary home until his death in 1790. Although the brick house where he lived in later life was torn down not long after he died, a steel structure within Independence National Historical Park outlines the spot where the house stood. The site also includes a replica of Franklin's printing office, a postal museum, and other displays and exhibits honoring his myriad accomplishments.

Several other landmarks celebrate this city's favorite son. The city-block-sized Franklin Institute is a hands-on museum and education center honoring Franklin's legacy and genius. A twenty-foot-tall statue of Franklin sits within the rotunda of the institute as part of the Benjamin Franklin National Memorial.

The majestic tree- and flag-lined Benjamin Franklin Parkway stretches from City Hall to the Philadelphia Museum of Art through the heart of the city. Two large traffic circles hold statuary art and elaborate water fountains, including the statue of

Benjamin Franklin Parkway, from the Philadelphia Museum of Art, 1930s

George Washington on horseback at Eakins Oval in front of the museum. The parkway also serves as a stage for fairs, parades, and other events, including the annual Fourth of July parade.

The steel-truss Benjamin Franklin Bridge spans the Delaware River from Philadelphia to Camden, New Jersey, and was the longest suspension bridge when it opened in 1926.

Benjamin Franklin Parkway at night

Above: *Benjamin Franklin Bridge*
Left: *July 4th Parade, Benjamin Franklin Parkway*

Mother Bethel A.M.E. Church, Philadelphia

RICHARD ALLEN AND THE
A.M.E. CHURCH

During the late 1800s, many of Philadelphia's black residents, both free and slave, joined white Christian congregations. Although black constituents were welcomed at many of the churches, they encountered much discrimination. In 1787, the African and African-American

Richard Allen (center) and other bishops of the A.M.E. Church

members of St. George's Methodist Episcopal Church withdrew after facing increasingly unfair treatment by the white leadership. Led by Richard Allen and Absalom Jones, the group purchased a lot on Sixth Street in Philadelphia and began construction of their own place of worship. The Bethel African Methodist Episcopal Church was dedicated in 1794 with twenty members and Allen as pastor. The denomination was formally organized as the African Methodist Episcopal Church (A.M.E.) in 1816, and Allen, a former slave, was elected its first bishop. The denomination grew rapidly, and it played a vital role in educating and providing aid to Africans and African Americans in the community. The church was also used as a stop on the Underground Railroad to help escaping slaves.

The current Bethel African Methodist Episcopal Church building on Sixth Street, the fourth on the site, was dedicated in 1890. Known as Mother Bethel, the church continues to serve a vibrant, mostly African-American community. The lower level of the building houses the Richard Allen Museum.

PHILADELPHIA MUSEUM OF ART

One of the largest and most important art museums in the United States, the Philadelphia Museum of Art was founded at the 1876 Centennial Exhibition. Construction on the current building, located at the western end of Benjamin Franklin Parkway, began in 1919, and it opened to the public nine years later.

Among its extensive permanent collection of paintings, sculptures, crafts, and other artwork from around the world, the museum is best known for its collections of Pennsylvania German art and the work of Thomas Eakins, the prominent Philadelphia artist. The Philadelphia Museum of Art also brings in fifteen to twenty special exhibitions each year. Typically, the museum brings in more than eight hundred thousand visitors annually.

The museum's main building and its steps are famous, too, for its role as a location in the film *Rocky* and two of its sequels.

Right: *East Plaza, Philadelphia Museum of Art*
Below: *Main facade, Philadelphia Museum of Art, 1930s*

THE PHILADELPHIA ORCHESTRA AND THE KIMMEL CENTER

The American Academy of Music in Philadelphia has been hosting opera and other performances since the majestic neo-Baroque facility opened on Broad Street in 1857. It served as the home of the Philadelphia Orchestra from the orchestra's founding in 1900 until 2001, when it moved to the modern Kimmel Center. The band shell on Benjamin Franklin Parkway was used for open-air concerts beginning in the early 1900s.

Designed and built specifically for the orchestra, the Kimmel Center for the Performing Arts is the city's latest state-of-the-art facility for concerts, educational activities, and recordings. Architect Rafael Viñoly and acoustician Russell Johnson designed two performance spaces: the 2,500-seat Verizon Hall for orchestral presentations, and the 650-seat Perelman Theater for chamber music concerts.

In addition to the serious works, the Kimmel Center hosts fun activities as well. The Summer Solstice Celebration presents music, dance, food, yoga, and juggling in a nineteen-hour marathon of lighthearted pleasure to welcome the return of summer.

American Academy of Music auditorium

Bandshell, Benjamin Franklin Parkway, 1920

Kimmel Center lobby

Left: *Kimmel Center exterior*
Below: *American Academy of Music, 1957*

Mummers Parade, 1909

Mummers Parade, 1909

Mummers Parade, 1916

Mummers Parade, 1916

Every New Year's Day in Philadelphia, thousands of performers dress in outlandish costumes and ride elaborate floats as part of the Mummers Parade—sometimes in bitterly cold weather. The Mummers are based on a tradition that dates back to 400 BC, when laborers marched with masks in the Roman Festival of Saturnalias.

The first official Mummers Parade in Philadelphia took place on January 1, 1901. The prize that year for best costume display was $1,725; today the total prize money is about $400,000. Still, the cash award might cover only part of the thousands of dollars that are spent on constructing the costumes and preparing for the event.

Mummer clubs work all year on their costumes and practice for the one-day event that draws large crowds along Broad Street as well as network TV viewers. The Mummers are categorized into four main groups: Comics, Fancies, String Bands, and Fancy Brigades. From a platform at City Hall, String Bands are judged on their musical performances as well as their costumes. Other costumes—inspired by the spirit of Momus, the ancient Greek god of mockery, ridicule, and scorn—offer commentaries on current events, culture, and politics. The Mummers Parade has not been without controversy, however, particularly with regard to the exclusion of women and people performing in blackface.

SOUTH PHILLY'S ITALIAN MARKET

Once the domain of the city's Italian population, South Philly is the site of the famous Italian Market, the oldest and largest working outdoor market in the United States. Early photographs show the Ninth Street market with the same busyness as today, if less orderly and with fewer gourmet shops. Then as now, vendors spilled onto the street and sold produce so fast that empty baskets and cartons were piled haphazardly or tossed aside aimlessly.

Though still heavily Italian, the market today offers cuisines of many cultures, and South Philly has become a diverse, multi-ethnic neighborhood. Many Asian families have moved into the area and opened their own stalls in the market.

The Italian Market is both a big draw for out-of-town tourists and a regular destination for the most discriminating gourmet cook. With more than one hundred merchants, the market presents a cornucopia of sights and smells. Included among the offerings are four cheese vendors, seven meat markets, four fish merchants, forty produce vendors, two pasta factories, four coffee shops, two bakeries for sweets, and two bakeries for Italian and

Italian Market, 1936

other breads. A veritable superstore, the market also has several cookware shops as well as merchants selling everything from lingerie and clothing to antiques and jewelry. The city's renowned Philly cheese steak sandwiches are served up at the legendary Geno's Steaks, on the corner of South Ninth Street and Passyunk Avenue.

Italian Market, 1915

Above: *Italian Market, 2007*
Left: *Geno's Steaks*

READING TERMINAL

Reading Terminal ad, circa 1889

During the great railroad era of the late nineteenth century, the major railroad companies competed to build architecturally extravagant stations in cities throughout the United States. In 1893, the Reading Railroad completed its magnificent palace at Twelfth and Market Streets in Philadelphia. A lithograph from the time boasted: "This terminal is the largest and most commodious of its kind in the world, and one of the most beautiful public buildings in America." The grand terminal featured a pink-and-white, eight-story office building.

As part of its plans for the new terminal, the Reading Railroad also purchased, for $1 million, the farmers' market that had existed on the site since the 1600s. On the lower level of the terminal, below the raised train platforms, seventy-eight thousand square feet of space—enough for eight hundred merchants—was offered up to vendors to sell food and other delights. Amish-made food products, fresh vegetables, flowers, and many prepared foods were sold in market stalls, at counters, and at restaurant tables.

Today, the Reading Terminal Market thrives as a tourist destination as well as a supplier of farm-fresh produce, and sections of the Reading Railroad Terminal have been incorporated as a stylish annex to the Pennsylvania Convention Center (PCC), built in the late 1990s. A National Historic Landmark, the terminal's

Reading Terminal, 1910s

train shed is now PCC's Grand Hall and Ballroom. The extensively redesigned and remodeled Reading Terminal Headhouse is now office space and additional meeting and ballroom facilities, and the upper levels supply more than two hundred additional rooms to the new Marriott Hotel, which is connected by a skywalk. Retail outlets on the concourse level are anchored by the Hard Rock Cafe.

With the Reading Terminal no longer serving rail traffic, Amtrak makes stops at 30th Street Station and in North Philly, and the local subway trains stop at 30th Street, Suburban Station (at JFK Boulevard and 16th Street), and Market Street East near Independence Park.

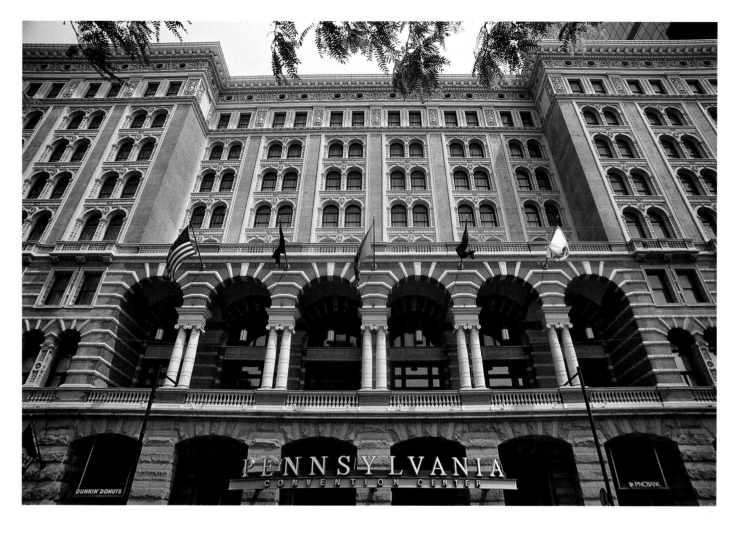

Above: *Pennsylvania Convention Center*
Left: *Reading Terminal Market*

Above: *30th Street Station, 1930s*

Right: *Aerial view of 30th Street Station, 1930s*

30TH STREET STATION

Pennsylvania Railroad War Memorial, 30th Street Station

30th Street Station, with Cira Centre in the background

Ranking behind only New York City's Penn Station, Philadelphia's 30th Street Station is the second-busiest passenger railroad terminal in the United States, with nearly four million boardings and alightings a year. The station is owned by Amtrak and houses Amtrak's corporate offices, but it is also one of three regional SEPTA rail hubs, and it serves New Jersey Transit.

Located on the banks of the Schuylkill River in West Philly, the 30th Street Station was built by the Pennsylvania Railroad in 1934. The art deco interior draws visitors to the elaborate ceiling in the cavernous concourse. The station's main information booth retains the old mechanical schedule board, with letters and numbers that flip into place to indicate arrivals and departures. A large bronze statue honors the Pennsylvania Railroad employees who

died in World War II. Created by Walker Hancock, the statue depicts the archangel Michael carrying a lifeless soldier, and engraved in the pedestal are the names of all 1,307 railroad employees who died in the war.

The station, now listed on the National Register of Historic Places, is within walking distance of Drexel University and the University of Pennsylvania. In 2005, the gleaming Cira Centre, a 437-foot-tall office building, opened next to the Amtrak station.

FAIRMOUNT PARK

Located on both banks of the Schuylkill River, Fairmount Park is one of the largest urban parks in the United States. In addition to its miles of hiking and biking trails and acres of open fields, the park contains the Philadelphia Zoo, the Horticulture Center, the Centennial Arboretum, the Mann Center for the Performing Arts, the Fairmount Water Works, and other landmarks. Boathouse Row, on the east bank of the river, consists of ten homes that serve as the jumping-off point for rowing and sculling competitions. Fairmount Park was the site of the city's Centennial Exhibition in 1876 to celebrate the one hundredth anniversary of the Declaration of Independence.

One of Philadelphia's most unusual attractions is the Japanese House (Shofuso), located on the grounds of the Horticultural Center in Fairmount Park. The sixteenth-century-style house and gardens were designed along the lines of what have been fitting for an upper-class, educated Japanese family of the period. The house has perfect symmetry, and the gardens are planted in authentic style for the house.

Fairmount Park, circa 1900

Centennial Exhibition, Fairmount Park, 1876

Numerous mansions are nestled within Fairmount Park, most of which are open to the public. During Christmas season, the Philadelphia Museum of Art offers candlelight tours of the mansions. The Mount Pleasant Mansion has enjoyed a 240-year history with many makeovers, including use as a German-style beer garden and, at another time, as a dairy that sold milk and ice cream. The grandest of the park's historic houses, the 4,700-square-foot Mount Pleasant recently underwent a much-needed $1.6 million restoration. The riverside estate was once owned by General Benedict Arnold.

Above: *Japanese House, Fairmount Park*
Left: *Family biking in Fairmount Park*

PHILADELPHIA-AREA COLLEGES AND UNIVERSITIES

Philadelphia and its surrounding counties are home to an abundance of prestigious institutions of higher education. Drexel University and the University of Pennsylvania make up "University City" in West Philly, and Temple University is located on Broad Street, just north of the city center. On the Main Line to the west of the city are Villanova University, Bryn Mawr College, Haverford College, and Immaculata University. Cheney and Lincoln Universities are historically black state institutions. Philadelphia metro-area colleges also include Cabrina, Eastern, Neumann, Rosemont, and St. Joseph's, among others.

The strong educational traditions of Pennsylvania's Quaker community are particularly evident at two small, liberal arts colleges located in Delaware County west of Philadelphia: Haverford College and Swarthmore College. Held in high regard for their academic excellence, they regularly rank among the top liberal arts schools in the nation.

Founded in 1833 as a men's school, Haverford is the oldest Quaker-founded college or university in the United States, although it no longer holds any religious affiliations; it has been coed since 1980. The school's values of individual responsibility, academic integrity, and cultural tolerance are reinforced by a student-supported Honor Code.

Parrish Hall, Swarthmore College

Postcard view of Parrish Hall, Swarthmore College, circa 1940

Swarthmore College, incorporated in 1864, admitted its first students, both men and women, in 1869. Also founded by members of the Religious Society of Friends, or Quakers, Swarthmore has been nonsectarian since early in the twentieth century. It is renowned for its honors program, and Swarthmore is one of the few liberal arts schools to offer an engineering program.

The two colleges are located on beautiful suburban grounds just a few miles from downtown Philadelphia, and both encompass large arboretums that are open to the public.

Haverford and Swarthmore have joined with the prestigious women's college nearby, Bryn Mawr, to form the Tri-College Consortium, which links the schools' academic programs, libraries, resources, and research facilities. Swarthmore College has a separate peace library, used by international researchers on peace and nonviolence.

Haverford College

Postcard view of Founders' Hall, Haverford College

Bryn Mawr College

Postcard view of Montgomery County Courthouse, Norristown

Postcard view of Main Street, Norristown, circa 1900

COUNTY SEATS AND SUBURBAN SPRAWL

Each of Pennsylvania's sixty-seven counties has a county seat, the town that holds the county court and government offices. Many of the state's county courthouses are monuments to the spread of wealth across Pennsylvania during the late 1700s and 1800s, as settlers moved west and north from the Lower Delaware Valley with the progress of industries related to iron mining, lumbering, coal mining, oil drilling, railroading, and the canal system.

Norristown is the county seat of Montgomery County in southeastern Pennsylvania, and site of the ornate Montgomery County Courthouse. Once a county of farmers, many of them Mennonites, Montgomery County is now home to wealthy business people, executives, and intellectuals from nearby Philadelphia. Around Norristown, suburban developments, shopping malls, and specialty markets have seemingly sprung up in every field. Some of the private homes in the area are among the largest and most expensive in the East. Norristown and its courthouse retain their historic charm as the city competes with the increasingly developed surroundings.

As in much of the United States, the boroughs of Pennsylvania have faced an uphill battle to keep their downtowns vibrant as commercial activity, particularly in the form of the ever-multiplying strip malls, has sprawled into the surrounding countryside. Although

Montgomery County Courthouse, Norristown

Pennsylvania has maintained an even population (growth of only 1.2 percent between 2000 and 2005), housing developments on former farmland proceed at a breathtaking rate. To cope, downtowns have transformed into centers for business offices, specialty shops, and art venues, some with greater success than others.

Above: *Historic District, Norristown*
Left: *Suburban development in Bucks County*

Washington at Valley Forge, *painting by Edward Percy Moran, 1911*

VALLEY FORGE

Battling disease, hunger, and bitter cold, the Continental Army, led by General George Washington, encamped at Valley Forge during the winter of 1777–1778, while British forces rested a mere eighteen miles away in Philadelphia, in much more comfortable surroundings. A year and a half after the Declaration of Independence, Washington's twelve-thousand-man army had grown by four times, but the general resisted urgings to attack the British, opting to allow his men to recuperate from the battles of the preceding months. To keep morale up in the harsh conditions at Valley Forge, Washington offered prizes for such accomplishments as the first regiment to build a structure and to the men who solved the problem of how to seal the roofs of their huts. The ragtag army also used the time for military drills and training. Although no battle was fought at Valley Forge, the Continental Army's ability to hold together and regroup through the difficult winter proved a turning point in the fight for independence.

The significance of Valley Forge in the struggle for independence only began to be recognized in the mid-1800s. By 1893, it was named Pennsylvania's first state park. Valley Forge remained in state hands until 1976, when it was transferred to the National Park System to become Valley Forge National Historical Park.

Visitors to Valley Forge National Historical Park can learn about the history of this pivotal event and of the Revolutionary War by exploring various monuments, Washington's headquarters, the grand drilling grounds, and the modern visitors' center. On frequent occasions, re-enactors help bring the experience to life, and the park also has a self-guided tour. The three thousand acres of rolling grassland include bike paths and horse trails for those pursuing leisure.

National Memorial Arch, Valley Forge National Historical Park

Re-enactor, Valley Forge National Historical Park

Postcard veiw of Delaware Water Gap

DELAWARE WATER GAP

Geologists surmise that the path of the Delaware River cutting through the Kittatinny Ridge was made over millions of years as water eroded through a fault or weakness in the ridge that runs north from Virginia through Pennsylvania and into New Jersey. As water cascades from the Pocono Plateau to the Delaware River Valley, numerous waterfalls have formed, including spectacular cascades such as Dingman's, Winona, and Bushkill falls.

Stretching north from the gap along the river is the Delaware Water Gap National Recreation Area. This stunning landscape has been the subject of painters and other artists since the nineteenth century, and it has long been a popular destination for canoeing and rafting on the Delaware River. The break in the mountains was also used as a path for railroad lines and, more recently, for Interstate 80 to speed cars and trucks across the river between Pennsylvania and New Jersey.

Above: *Dingman's Falls, Delaware Water Gap National Recreation Area*

Left: *Aerial view of Delaware Water Gap National Recreation Area and Interstate 80*

BETHLEHEM

Settled in 1741 by immigrants from the Moravian region of what is today the Czech Republic, the city of Bethlehem remains a center of Moravian activity and culture in eastern Pennsylvania. The original Sisters House has been maintained to its historic appearance and now houses a Moravian museum. Other Bethlehem sites—including Moravian College, the Moravian Theological Seminary, an eighteenth-century apothecary, and a Moravian church—serve the religious group as well as attracting visitors to the historic city. A restored crafts and industrial site, the Colonial Industrial Quarter, displays the business and manufacturing of early Moravians.

The eighteenth-century engraving shows the burgeoning Moravian community along the banks of the Lehigh River in Pennsylvania's then-undeveloped countryside. By the early twentieth century, Bethlehem was a leading industrial center, with row houses lining the hilly city streets.

The Bethlehem Steel Company, once the second-largest producer of steel in the United States (behind the Pittsburgh-based U.S. Steel), was founded in South Bethlehem in 1857 and operated until the late 1990s, when the company filed for bankruptcy.

Bethlehem street, 1935

View of Bethlehem, engraving by Paul Sandby, 1761

Central Moravian Church, 1937

The Bethlehem plant was a major source of jobs for the community, and its closure had devastating effects on the region's economy.

Bethlehem is still an attraction for tourists to the Lehigh Valley. During the Christmas holidays, peace advocates sponsor a quiet walk from the nearby borough of Nazareth to Bethlehem. In the city, Christmas carols ring out from nightly programs at a cozy, candlelit stone church. Many visitors come to see the crèche, which shows the countryside of Palestine on a starlit night. On the indoor set, as the Christmas story is told, the light guiding the shepherds moves across the landscape to Bethlehem's stable.

Above: *Bethlehem street*

Central Moravian Church

Below: *Christmas lights on Main Street*

North 7th Street, 1940s

Downtown pedestrian mall

North 10th Street, 1985

North 7th Street, city center

ALLENTOWN

Outside the boundaries of Philadelphia and Pittsburgh, Pennsylvania is a state of hundreds of small cities, towns (or boroughs, as they are officially known in the state), and villages scattered across the countryside. In the early 1800s, towns served as commerce centers for farm communities, but as industry expanded and suburbs sprouted in the 1900s, cities grew and increasingly became the commercial centers for the greater region. Once large factories, the interstate highway system, and housing developments expanded into the suburbs, however, retailers and residents moved to the outskirts of urban areas, and Pennsylvania's inner cities lost much of their vibrancy.

In the 1990s, great effort was expended to revitalize Pennsylvania's cities and bring people and commercial activity back to the downtown areas. Closed department stores were transformed into specialty shops, and art galleries and restaurants were opened on once-deserted streets, fostering a renaissance of sorts. In Allentown, North Seventh Street has once again become a vibrant thoroughfare in the center of the city, and the downtown shopping district has a new pedestrian-friendly layout.

Aerial view of Easton

EASTON

Bethlehem, Allentown, and Easton form a trio of cities in the Lehigh Valley. Together they constitute Pennsylvania's third-largest metropolitan area, and one of the state's fastest growing communities. Easton, the smallest of the three cities, is situated on the New Jersey border, northeast of Bethlehem. The two aerial photos illustrate the growth at this juncture of the Lehigh and Delaware rivers. As in many Pennsylvania towns and cities, Easton's downtown plaza features a memorial to soldiers who died fighting for the country. The plaza remains a gathering place in downtown.

Aerial view of Easton

Soldiers and Sailors Monument, Easton, Pa.

Left: *Postcard view of Soldiers and Sailors Monument*
Below: *Soldiers and Sailors Monument*

READING

The city of Reading was built on the profits of the booming anthracite coal and railroad industries of the nineteenth century. Its legendary Reading Railroad carried the "black gold" from the mining regions of northeastern Pennsylvania to be distributed throughout the state and beyond. Following years of decline that came with the end of the coal era in the middle of the twentieth century, the city worked to reinvent itself by introducing outlet shopping as a tourist industry and proclaiming itself "The Original Outlet Capital of the World."

Today, spacious Penn Square in the city center has a new look, adorned with flowers, brick walkways, and renovated historic buildings. The most prominent building on the wide Penn Square is the Abraham Lincoln Hotel, which was built in 1930 and recently restored. The grandfather of our nation's sixteenth president was born and raised in Berks County before the family moved west.

Elsewhere in downtown Reading, a former lens-crafting factory has been transformed into a comprehensive arts and cultural center known as GoggleWorks. In addition to a theater, classrooms, and many other facilities, about forty artists have studios in the converted factory. The public can see artists at work, as well as view finished art on display, ranging from acrylics and watercolors to jewelry, with a wide gamut of art forms in between.

Reading's most distinctive feature is the Japanese Pagoda, located atop Mount Penn and visible from around the city. Built in 1908, the pagoda is being refurbished in preparation for its one hundredth anniversary and will include a coffee shop and gift store.

PENN SQUARE, LOOKING WEST, READING, PA.

Postcard view of Penn Square, early 1900s

Japanese Pagoda, Reading

Postcard view of Penn Square, 1940s

Penn Square, with Abraham Lincoln Hotel in distance

Mule-drawn canal boat on the Delaware Canal, near Narrowsville

CANALS

As early as the days of William Penn, planners and engineers were well aware of the benefits of water transport compared with travel by covered wagon. To complement the state's vast river system, a network of canals was built across Pennsylvania around the turn of the nineteenth century. Canal building was labor intensive, as they had to be hand-dug by thousands of workers using picks and shovels and blasting powder.

Construction of the seventy-five-mile Union Canal, which linked the Susquehanna and Schuylkill rivers between Middletown and Reading, began in the early 1790s, but lack of funding delayed the project; it was completed in 1828. Nicknamed the "Golden Link," the towpath canal linked the lumber and coal mining regions of central Pennsylvania with Philadelphia until the canal closed in the 1880s. Today, a restored portion can be explored at the Union Canal Towpath Trail near Reading. An engineering marvel when completed in 1827, the Union Canal Tunnel, near Lebanon, is the oldest standing transportation tunnel in the United States.

The Delaware and Hudson Canal, which also opened in 1828, helped to link northeastern Pennsylvania's Coal Region with New York City and other markets on the eastern seaboard. Beginning on the Rondout Creek near Kingston, New York, the canal ran southwest to the Delaware River at Port Jervis, where it crossed the river to Lackawaxen, Pennsylvania, via the Delaware Aqueduct. The aqueduct was designed in the 1840s by John A. Roebling, who later engineered the Brooklyn Bridge. Today, the 535-foot restored aqueduct is the oldest existing wire-suspension bridge in the United States. The historic site accommodates automobile and pedestrian traffic.

Mule-drawn canal boat ride, Delaware Canal State Park

From Lackawaxen, the D&H Canal traveled along the Lackawaxen River to Honesdale. At Honesdale, the canal was replaced by a gravity railroad for the final stretch to Carbondale, because the terrain was too steep for locks. The gravity rail was integral in transporting coal from the anthracite mines near Carbondale to the canal system.

The Lehigh Canal connected the Lehigh Valley with the Delaware River, and it functioned as a means of transportation until 1932, making it the last active towpath canal in the nation. The emergence of the railroads had rendered canal transport all but obsolete by the end of the nineteenth century, although the Lehigh Coal and Navigation Company utilized the Lehigh and Delaware Canals for coal transportation through the 1920s.

Today, a restored, sixty-mile section of the Delaware Canal from Easton to Bristol is a popular destination for tourists and for outdoor recreation. Visitors can ride mule-drawn canal boats through Delaware Canal State Park from the town of New Hope.

Musician entertaining tourists on canal boat ride, Delaware Canal State Park

Mauch Chunk and Lehigh River, 1896.

JIM THORPE

Broadway, Looking West from Susquehanna Street, Mauch Chunk, Pa

Postcard view of Broadway, early 1900s

Once known as the "Switzerland of Pennsylvania," the town of Jim Thorpe is pinched in amid the mountains of the Lehigh River Valley. Broadway runs through the main part of town, a tourists' treasure. Bed-and-breakfasts, restaurants, and quaint shops hug the street.

Originally known as Mauch Chunk, the town was renamed for the Native American athlete James Francis Thorpe, considered by many to be the greatest athlete of the twentieth century. At the 1912 Olympic Games in Stockholm, he won gold medals in the pentathlon and decathlon. Thorpe was also a two-time All-American while playing collegiate football for the Carlisle Indian Industrial School, and he went on to play professional baseball and football.

The city was rechristened in Thorpe's honor following his death in 1953 in an effort to attract tourism to the picturesque town. A memorial honors him there.

Today, the town of Jim Thorpe is a launching point for kayaking, canoeing, and rafting in the Lehigh Gorge and for hiking in the mountains. In the heyday of the railroad and coal industries, the town served as a vacation spot for the wealthy. Railroad magnate Asa Packer built a mansion overlooking the town; it is now a fine Victorian home museum. In addition to enjoying the shops, restaurants, and mansion, visitors to the town will be intrigued by the jail, now a museum, and the 1869 Gothic Revival Episcopal church on Race Street, which offers tours.

Above: *Jim Thorpe and Lehigh River*
Left: *Broadway*

EPHRATA CLOISTER

During the eighteenth century, many religious sects persecuted in Europe found their way to William Penn's "Holy Experiment," a colony established on the principles of religious and political freedom in the New World. Amish, Mennonites, various Baptist sects, Moravians, and others cleared lands for farming and to build their places of worship. Cloistered communal groups also took root in several areas. One such group, in Lancaster County, grew around German-born Conrad Beissel. In the 1730s, Beissel left his Conestoga Brethren Congregation near present-day Lancaster and settled into a hermit's life along the Cocalico Creek. He was soon joined by a following of believers seeking his guidance and inspiration.

Under Beissel's leadership, the numbers grew until the seekers formed a community, which they called the Solitary. The members of the group were rebaptized, and they embraced pacifism and the monastic lifestyle; many became celibate. Those in the community who remained married were known as the Householders and lived in separate facilities. Though the group did not have common property, they practiced mutual aid within the community and charity in the surrounding neighborhoods.

The Ephrata community grew to as many as four hundred members during the late 1700s. They built their own dwellings as well as a print shop, where printing was both a business and part of the mission. Among the books published were several editions of the New Testament; the book of Mennonite martyrs, *Martyrs Mirror*; and the community's hymnals. Beissel also wrote lyrics and musical scores, and the members of the Cloister performed four-, five-, and six-part a cappella music.

Although Beissel died in 1768, the Society continued on. In 1814, the remaining members incorporated themselves as the Seventh Day German Baptist Church, which survived until 1934.

Saron (Sisters' House) and Saal (Meetinghouse), Ephrata Cloister, 1936

The Ephrata Cloister site has been administered by the Pennsylvania Historical and Museum Commission since 1941. Thousands of visitors come to the site every year, particularly during the holiday candlelit tours. Interpreters in period costume offer guided tours of the grounds year-round, and a museum and visitors' center offer additional information on the cloister and its original community. When entering the Saal, or large worship room, a guide will warn visitors: "Be careful. The doorways were made very low to encourage humility."

WPA promotional poster, late 1930s

Kitchen at Ephrata Cloister, with models in Cloister attire

Saron and Saal, Ephrata Cloister

LANCASTER

The city of Lancaster, seat of its namesake county, served as the Pennsylvania state capital from 1799 to 1812. During that period, the state offices were housed in the Georgian-style brick building at the northwest corner Penn Square on King Street. Built in 1795–1997 for county offices, the structure later served as Lancaster City Hall and was restored to its original design in 1924. Today it is home to the Lancaster Cultural History Museum (formerly the Heritage Center Museum).

Penn Square is the hub of downtown Lancaster, and for more than 130 years the square has been anchored by the Soldiers and Sailors Monument. The monument was dedicated on July 4, 1874, as a tribute to the residents of Lancaster County who fought in the Civil War and other conflicts.

On the southeast side of Penn Square is the elaborate Watt and Shand department store, built in 1898. The department store closed in 1995, and the structure is being partially torn down and transformed into a hotel and convention center as part of redevelopment efforts in the city center.

West King Street, 1920s

Central Market, 1942

Soldiers and Sailors Monument, Penn Square

Lancaster's Central Market, located just west of the Cultural History Museum, is America's oldest publicly owned, continuously operated farmers' market. The site has been used as a market since the 1730s, and the current Romanesque Revival–style Central Market building was constructed in 1889. The market is a favorite destination of residents and visitors alike, and it is a great place to buy produce and other goods directly from Lancaster County farms.

Penn Square, toward North Queen Street

Amish produce stand, Central Market

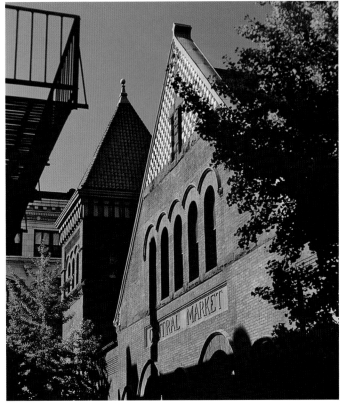

Central Market exterior

Mennonite buggies in church yard, Lancaster County, 1942

Amish women preparing Sunday dinner, Lancaster County, 1957

THE AMISH

The Old Order Amish of Lancaster County have provided travel and vacation planners with one of the strongest magnets in America. Hotels, markets, and quilt and craft shops have sprung up around Lancaster city and the towns of Bird-in-Hand, Quarryville, Leola, New Holland, and Intercourse. Dozens of restaurants serve Pennsylvania Dutch food, and museums have been established to explain and celebrate the Amish lifestyle.

The Amish were formed in 1693 when a group led by Jacob Amman broke off from the Mennonites, a Christian Anabaptist denomination established in Europe during the sixteenth century. The two sects still share many of the same beliefs, such as adult baptism, pacifism, and basic Bible doctrines, and they share the history recorded in *Martyrs Mirror*, which tells of the persecution and death of many early Anabaptists in Europe, who practiced illegal (by church and state law) rebaptism.

While thirteen Dutch Mennonite families first came to Germantown (now in north Philadelphia) in response to William Penn's "Holy Experiment" in the 1680s, the Amish didn't arrive in Pennsylvania until the years between 1727 and 1770, after many Mennonites had moved west into Lancaster County. Word of the rich soils along the Conestoga River soon reached the Amish, and they opted to settle in the area with Mennonites and other immigrants. In the years that followed, the Amish and Mennonites prospered, taking advantage of some of America's most fertile soils.

WPA promotional poster, late 1930s

Amish buggies and barn raising, Lancaster County

Young Amish women, Lancaster County

Young Amish couple with chaperone in open buggy,
Lancaster County, 1957

As available farmland for their children and grandchildren has dwindled in Lancaster County over the past several decades, the Amish have moved into other areas of Pennsylvania where they can buy farms. Rather than moving away, others have become entrepreneurs in the building, crafts, furniture-making, and machine trades. Across the state, the Amish have developed close-knit communities, with one-room schools within walking distance. Of the 198,000 Amish in the United States, about 47,000 live in Pennsylvania.

The horse-and-buggy transportation, mule-powered field machinery, and plain dress distinguish the Amish today. While the Amish have retained a nineteenth-century lifestyle, with women clad in solid-color dresses and men all in black, most Mennonites have accepted new technologies and "worldly" dress.

A slow drive through Lancaster County's countryside offers an opportunity to experience a time long since past in most areas of the United States. You can enjoy the industrious work of Amish farmers and craftspeople, free of the noise of gas and electric engines—other than those of the ever-present tour buses.

Amish couple in open buggy, Lancaster County

Amish farm, Lancaster County

FARMING AND AGRICULTURE

The rolling hills and fertile valleys of "Penn's Woods" are conducive to farming plots of all shapes and sizes, and agriculture has been a mainstay of Pennsylvania's landscape and economy since the earliest peoples settled in the area. The staple crops of the Lenni Lenape in the east and the Monongahela tribes in the west included corn, beans, and squash. Early German and Swedish settlers brought new crops such as wheat, oats, barley, and other grains as well as fruits and vegetables, and they introduced crop rotation to help keep the land fertile. Most early Pennsylvania farms had a few pigs, chickens, a milk cow or two, some ducks or sheep, and large vegetable gardens—enough for canning and the family's daily needs, and a little extra to take to market to sell for cash.

The development of mechanized equipment and techniques in the nineteenth century led to a revolution in farming, and the new canal and railroad systems allowed farmers to get their products to

PENNSYLVANIA

WPA promotional poster, late 1930s

many more markets. The advent of electrical power and the arrival of tractor-powered machinery in the first half of the twentieth century further improved life for the Pennsylvania farmer.

Farming remains a major component of the Pennsylvania economy in the twenty-first century. According to the Department of Agriculture, there are more than fifty-eight thousand active farms covering 7.7 million acres. While corporate farms have made inroads, most Pennsylvania farms are still family-owned.

Dairying is the largest agricultural industry in the state. Today's large diary farms have milking parlors that can take milk from as many as five hundred cows; most activities are computerized and nearly automatic. Cows are fed rations just right for their optimum production, formulated and dispensed from computerized settings. Most farms grow their own corn, wheat, and alfalfa crops, which are mixed with feed supplements for the dairy or beef herds.

Early Pennsylvania farmer

Milking parlor at dairy farm, Shippensburg

Aerial view of farm, Northumberland County

Farm equipment hall, State Farm Show

Champion steer, Farm Show, 1979

THE FARM SHOW AND COUNTY FAIRS

Every January since 1917, farmers from across the state gather in Harrisburg with their best livestock, crops, and produce to take part in the Pennsylvania Farm Show. The eight-day event attracts half a million visitors every year, and some ten thousand exhibitors come to compete for prizes in livestock, craft, art, and produce categories. Located in eleven connected buildings and three arenas on twenty-five acres, the Farm Show is the largest indoor agricultural event in the country and has earned national and international recognition as one of the best agricultural exhibitions.

In rural Pennsylvania, it's not summer without a day at the county fair. More than a hundred county and community fairs take place throughout the state between June and October every year.

Large and small, these fairs provide ample opportunities for entertainment and good eating. Ferris wheels and other amusement rides, midway games and prizes, and outdoor concerts offer fun for all ages, from morning to night. From funnel cakes and cotton candy to pierogies and cheese steaks, there are tasty delights a-plenty. For farmers and gardeners, the livestock- and produce-judging is highly competitive, and the winners often go on to the statewide Farm Show in Harrisburg.

The first county fair in America was held at York, Pennsylvania, in 1765. Today, the York Fair is held on seven acres and remains one of the largest and finest fairs in the country. It has pony-cart races, tractor and auto events, and one of the largest midways among all Pennsylvania fairs.

Show cow entries, Farm Show, Harrisburg

Food stands, Wayne County Fair

Ferris wheel and midway rides, Lebanon County Fair

Hershey's Chocolate World entrance

HERSHEY

One might bypass other towns along central Pennsylvania's Route 422, but Hershey can't be overlooked; it is not only a sight to see, but something to smell. For chocolate lovers, the aroma emanating from the Hershey factory is overpoweringly alluring.

Founded by Milton S. Hershey in 1894, the Hershey Chocolate Company began as a subsidiary of Milton's Lancaster Caramel Company. By 1900, he had sold off the caramel company to focus on chocolate, and in 1903, he built a new factory in the town of Derry Church—later renamed Hershey. The affordable, mass-produced chocolates were a huge hit, and the company's flagship Hershey bar and the Hershey's Kiss (introduced in 1907) quickly became American icons. The Hershey Company grew to become the largest chocolate producer in the United States.

The town of Hershey, an amusement park, and elaborate homes were built around Hershey's chocolate factory in the early 1900s. The factory, located on Chocolate Avenue, offered tours, and the overwhelming popularity of the tours led the company to open a separate Chocolate World in 1973. Visitors can board a moving car to take them through a simulation of the chocolate-making process, from the cocoa plots of Africa to final packaging. The tour is free—which is good, because you'll want to save your pennies for the shops, where all of Hershey's chocolate products and other merchandise are available for sale.

Hershey chocolate factory

Postcard view of Chocolate Avenue, Hershey

Adjacent to Chocolate World is Hersheypark, an amusement park that the company opened in 1907. Originally open only to employees, the park offered picnic facilities, a bandstand, and boating on the nearby Spring Creek. When Hersheypark became a public attraction, new rides were added almost annually, from carousels to wild roller coasters, establishing Hersheypark's place as a state-of-the-art thrill-seekers' paradise. In the water ride section, the Tidal Force ends in a million-gallon water spray. The Comet is a classic wooden coaster, and the Storm Runner coaster has a rocketlike beginning. And, of course, there are plenty of Hershey Kisses to eat along the way. ZooAmerica, next door to the park, is an eleven-acre zoo with more than two hundred animals from all over the world.

In addition to providing attractions for the amusement of residents and tourists, the philanthropic activities of Milton Hershey and his wife, Catherine, led to the founding of the Hershey Industrial School, in 1909, as a free educational facility for orphaned boys. Now known as the Milton Hershey School, it provides free education from pre-kindergarten to twelfth grade for youths from low-income or socially stressed families of all races and ethnicities. Originally open only to white boys, today more than forty percent of the school's fourteen hundred girls and boys are African American or Hispanic. The proceeds from the entertainment and chocolate businesses go to the Hershey Trust, which funds the Milton Hershey School, in keeping with the founder's will.

Postcard view of Hersheypark pool

Hershey Industrial School

Founders Hall and Milton Hershey School, Hershey

SCENE IN HERSHEY PARK

Postcard view of Hersheypark pavilion

Sidewinder coaster, Hersheypark

HARRISBURG AND ITS
MARKET SQUARE

Few center cities have experienced the transformation that has occurred in Harrisburg's Market Square in recent decades. More than a century ago, the large, open area was filled with crude market stalls surrounded by horses and wagons (and mud and foul smells). When the market was moved to other locations in the city about a century past, new buildings, including a theater, began to fill the outer parts of the square. Following the exodus from the city to the suburbs in the 1960s and 1970s, much of Market Square was vacated. City Hall remained open, as did a furniture store and the Presbyterian Church, but most of the buildings were boarded up, and in the evenings the square had few pedestrians.

Then came the renaissance of the 1990s, when the unused buildings of Market Square fell to demolition crews. Rising out of the rubble were stately, modern structures: the Hilton Hotel, the Dauphin Deposit bank, the Keystone Insurance high-rise, and most recently, Market Place. At the turn of this century, restaurants started to open at a rapid pace north and east from the square on Second and Market Streets; there are now more than thirty eateries on Second Street's "Restaurant Row." Just off the square, the Whitaker Center for Science and the Arts opened its first-class concert hall, I-Max theater, and extensive hands-on science center. The shops of Strawberry Square—a modern office and retail structure opposite the capitol building and one block from Market Square—expanded into restored historic shops along Walnut, Third, and Market Streets. Today, Harrisburg has become a travelers' destination featuring a lively downtown with cultural and culinary delights, the State Capitol, the National Civil War Museum, the National Fire Museum, and a thriving farmers' market, the historic Broad Street Market.

City Island, on the Susquehanna River, is accessible from downtown by the pedestrian Walnut Street Bridge and the Market Street Bridge. The island is home to the ballpark of the minor league baseball club, the Harrisburg Senators, as well as other sports and recreational activities.

Postcard view of Market Square, 1860

High-rises and Market Square, Harrisburg

Postcard view of Market Square, Harrisburg, early 1900s

Harrisburg skyline from City Island, Commerce Bank Park in foreground

State Capitol, 1907

The State Capitol
Harrisburg, Pa.

Aerial view of State Capitol complex, circa 1940

Fountain at the State Capitol

Family in horse-drawn carriage at the State Capitol

THE STATE CAPITOL:
A "PALACE OF ART"

When Pennsylvania's Capitol building was dedicated in 1906, President Theodore Roosevelt called the American Beaux-Arts structure "the handsomest building I ever saw." Sitting on a rise in midtown Harrisburg, with the wide State Street boulevard leading to it from the east and west, the ornate classicism rises in bold relief. Governor Samuel W. Pennypacker oversaw the building's construction, and the building's architect was thirty-six-year-old Joseph M. Huston. Envisioning a "palace of art," Huston commissioned Pennsylvania artists to contribute to the decor, inside and out.

The green terra-cotta dome, modeled after the dome of St. Peter's Basilica in Rome, is topped by a female figure, "Commonwealth," sculpted by Roland Hinton. The two-ton bronze doors, which can be moved with a touch of a finger, were designed by George Grey Barnard, who also sculpted the white marble figures framing the exterior steps. When the sculptures were first exhibited, they stunned the European art world. Art critics compared Barnard to Phidias, Michelangelo, and Velazquez. One critic wrote that Barnard was a "master of light and shade."

Right: *Aerial view of State Capitol complex*

Capitol Rotunda, 1906

Restored Capitol Rotunda

Inside the capitol's awe-inspiring rotunda, the walls and ceiling are adorned with gold leaf, white marble, and glittering crystal. Four thirty-eight-foot murals painted by Philadelphia artist Edwin Austin Abbey represent *Law, Art, Science,* and *Religion.* Within the dome, sixteen ribs of gold, red, and blue emanate from the central gold stars on a blue background. The rotunda's floor is of handmade tiles by the renowned Bucks County ceramicist, Henry Mercer.

The art throughout the capitol complex incorporates symbols familiar to Pennsylvanians and reflects the themes of justice, peace, and religion. Edwin Abbey's gigantic murals in the House of Representatives depict events such as *Penn's Treaty with the Indians* and the reading of the Declaration of Independence; the centerpiece, *The Apotheosis,* depicts men in pursuit of science, law, and other vocations under an enthroned goddess representing the

Commonwealth. William B. Van Ingen's exquisite stained-glass windows are on display in the Senate chamber and the dome ceiling above the Supreme Court room.

Remarkable for the time, much of the artwork in the capitol was painted by a woman, Violet Oakley. Murals by all of the artists were huge, in both size and number, and Oakley's no less so. Encircling the mahogany-paneled Governor's Reception Room are sixteen murals that portray the history and persecution of religious groups that broke from the Church of England, centering on Quakers and the life of William Penn. Oakley's *Divine Law* mural in the Supreme Court room features the words "wisdom" and "love" in a kind of puzzlegram. Above the speaker's chair in the Senate chamber, her *International Understanding and Unity* represents the uniting of people of all races, ages, and stations in life. In all, Oakley painted forty-three murals for the capitol.

Stained-glass dome by William Van Ingen, Supreme Court, State Capitol

Governor's Reception Room, circa 1906

House of Representatives hall, State Capitol

Divine Law, by Violet Oakley, Supreme Court room

Bridges across the Susquehanna at Harrisburg.

SUSQUEHANNA RIVER BRIDGES

early a mile wide at some points, the Susquehanna River was a barrier to the westward movement of the young nation. An early ferry crossing was established by John Harris in the 1730s, and Harris Ferry, then part of Lancaster County, would later become Harrisburg, part of a newly created Dauphin County.

The Susquehanna was a challenge to bridge builders of the nineteenth and twentieth centuries. Several different types of spans were attempted over the years. The first crossing from Harrisburg's Market Street to the west bank of the river was a covered toll bridge, known as the Camel Back Bridge, completed in 1817. After several reconstructions, the wooden bridge was finally washed away by the river in 1902 and was replaced by a steel bridge. The current Market Street Bridge, a stone-faced concrete-arch bridge, was constructed between 1926 and 1928.

Postcard view of Camel Back Bridge at Market Street

Old Rockville Bridge

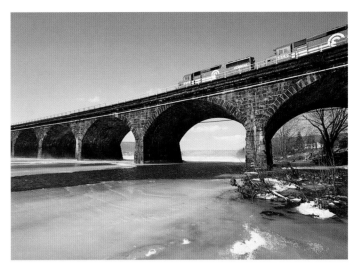

Rockville Bridge in winter

Paddlewheel boat at Market Street Bridge

Just north of Harrisburg city, the Rockville Bridge was originally a single-track wooden structure, built by the Pennsylvania Railroad in 1849. It was destroyed by a tornado and replaced by an iron truss bridge, in 1877, which had two tracks. The current stone-arch bridge enjoyed its one hundredth birthday in 2002. It is 3,830 feet long and has forty-eight spans, each seventy feet wide. In 1972, when Hurricane Agnes sent the Susquehanna River fifteen feet above flood stage, a coal train was set on the bridge to help stabilize it. Although the river lost many of its wooden bridges, Rockville stood firm. On another occasion, however, in 1997, a pier crumbled, and four carloads of coal dumped into the river.

The river crossing between Columbia and Wrightsville, downriver of Harrisburg, has been spanned by several structures, dating back to an 1814 covered bridge. A second covered bridge followed in the 1830s, only to be burned by Union troops during the Civil War. After a third wooden span was destroyed during an 1896 hurricane, a steel-truss bridge was erected to carry both rail and highway traffic. It served as a railroad bridge into the 1950s and was torn down in 1964. The current concrete Columbia-Wrightsville Bridge was constructed next to the railroad bridge in 1930 to accommodate the increasing automobile traffic. Today, all that remains of the steel railroad bridge are its stone pillars.

WRIGHT'S FERRY MANSION

Built along the Susquehanna River in what is now Columbia, the house of James Wright and his daughter, Susanna, marks the location of an eighteenth-century ferry crossing for the broad Susquehanna. Wright's Ferry Mansion stands alone today, telling the story of a few Quakers who ventured west from Chester into this wild region. The restored 1738 house contains a superb collection of period decorative arts and furnishings. The town of Columbia also features many later historic houses, a farmers' market, and the National Watch and Clock Museum. Wright's Ferry Mansion is said to have tunnels that were used as escape routes to the river for the Underground Railroad.

Below: *Wright's Ferry Mansion*

Above: *Wright's Ferry Mansion restored interior*

Postcard view of Market Street, Millersburg

Market Square, Millersburg

MILLERSBURG AND ITS FERRY

North of Harrisburg on the Susquehanna River lies Millersburg, a vibrant small town with a central square featuring war monuments, grassy areas, and a gazebo, like many Pennsylvania towns. But Millersburg has another treasure: the only ferry that continues to operate on the Susquehanna. Its exact date of origin is unknown, but in 1826, a sheriff's sale transferred Daniel Miller's propriety reserve and ferry rights to David Kramer, who did establish a ferry.

Passing through a string of ownerships, the ferry was nearly shut down in the 1980s because it was too expensive to operate, but in 1990 the ferry was bought by a local bank and deeded to the Millersburg Chamber of Commerce. It continues to run daily during favorable weather in spring, summer, and fall. It carries up to four cars and fifty people, and it can be rented in the evenings for concerts, weddings, or dinners on the river. The ferry service has two boats, which frequently pass each other on the mile-long voyage.

Millersburg ferry

Gettysburg 50th Reunion, 1913

GETTYSBURG

The bloodiest battle of the Civil War resulted from an unexpected meeting of Confederate troops and the Union cavalry near Gettysburg in Adams County, Pennsylvania. The cavalry was scouting for General John Buford, while the rebels, under General A. P. Hills, were searching for supplies. Dismayed by the chance meeting, General Hills sent his troops quickly toward Gettysburg. General Buford, surveying the landscape from a church tower, concluded that the contours of the land provided for good defenses, and he ordered the Union troops to form a defensive line. Hearing of the encounter, Confederate General Robert Lee ordered all of his men forward to Gettysburg.

Skirmishes and fierce fighting ensued as tens of thousands of troops amassed in the days that followed the chance meeting on July 1, 1863. On the first day alone, seven thousand Confederates were wounded, killed, or taken prisoner; the Union casualties were even greater in number. Both sides brought in reinforcements and supplies during the night and established battle lines. While the Union generals decided to stay in a defensive position on Cemetery Hill and wait for the Confederates to move, General Lee, against the wishes of his second-in-command, ordered his troops to attack the center of the Union line, moving uphill. Following several hours of opening cannon fire, heard as far away as Washington, D.C., bands of Confederate soldiers—twelve thousand of them—advanced on the Union position. The rebels failed to penetrate the Union lines in hand-to-hand fighting, and thousands perished.

Pickett's Charge, Gettysburg, 1863

Gettysburg battle re-enactment

Pickett's Charge, as the massive assault came to be known, was disastrous for the Confederate side, and Gettysburg proved to be a turning point in the war in favor of the Union. In all, fifty-four thousand warriors from both sides were killed, captured, or went missing during the vicious three-day encounter. Many of the dead were relocated to the Soldiers' National Cemetery on the south side of town. It was at the cemetery's dedication ceremony on November 19, 1863, that President Abraham Lincoln delivered his legendary Gettysburg Address.

Efforts to preserve the battlefield as a monument began almost immediately, with the formation of the Gettysburg Battlefield Memorial Association in 1864. In 1895, the federal government purchased the land and established the Gettysburg National Military Park.

Veterans from both sides of the conflict convened at Gettysburg in the summer of 1913 for the fiftieth anniversary of the battle. More than fifty thousand former soldiers arrived at the Great Camp set up for the gathering, with former foes recalling together the fateful events of July 1863.

Today, the six-thousand-acre Gettysburg National Military Park features miles of roads and walking paths that take you to various sites and monuments. A 360-degree cyclorama painting at the visitors' center illustrates the movements of the Union and Confederate troops during the three days of fighting. The key events of the battle are re-enacted by Civil War imitators, who replicate the clothing, weapons, and accessories of the soldiers who fought there more than 140 years ago.

Below: *Bicyclists touring Gettysburg National Military Park*

Above: *York city center, 1920s*
Right: *West Market Street, circa 1978*

York County Court House, East Market Street   *Fluhrer Building, West Market Street*

YORK

Of south-central Pennsylvania's three major cities—Lancaster, Harrisburg, and York—the "White Rose City" is the heavy lifter in manufacturing. York is home to some of the largest manufacturers of U.S.-made products. Harley-Davidson, York Barbells, York International (the largest domestic producer of HVAC units), Caterpillar, and American Hydro are just a few of the corporations with factories in or near the city. Earlier in its history, the city hosted the Continental Congress for a period during the Revolutionary War, and briefly served as the continental capital. It is the seat of its namesake county.

The manufacturing base and other financial benefactors have encouraged York's vibrancy with gifts to preserve the city's history and to foster the arts. The historic York Strand Theatre brings to the area internationally renowned music and theater talent. Artists have been commissioned to paint the city's history, personalities, and specialties in numerous murals throughout the city. Art galleries have emerged in the heart of the city. York and its namesake county boasts one of Pennsylvania's most active library systems. A visit to the new library, a tour of the city's murals, a gallery walk, or the walking tour of historic buildings will foster appreciation for the city's contributions to our nation's heritage.

Breaker boys, Pennsylvania Coal Company, South Pittston, 1911
Photo by Lewis Hine

ANTHRACITE COAL MINING

In the nineteenth and early twentieth centuries, anthracite coal, or "black gold," spurred the industrial prosperity of northeastern Pennsylvania's Coal Region. The hard, high-energy, efficient, clean-burning coal was first discovered here in 1790, and the first anthracite-fueled iron furnace was built on the Schuylkill River in 1795. Commercial mining operations began shortly thereafter, and the industry reached its peak in the 1910s. Anthracite was used as heating fuel for most homes in the northeastern United States by the late 1800s, and it helped to thrust the railroad industry forward.

Breakers, like the one shown in the historic photo, carried the mined coal over spikes to break it up, at which point the coal was pulled over several screens to separate the different-sized pieces.

Coal breaker, Scranton

Eckley Miners' Village

Young children, known as "breaker boys," were also employed to sift rocks from the coal.

As the mining industry prospered and cities and towns grew throughout the Coal Region, they also had to weather many calamities. Mining was (and still is) dangerous work, and many hundreds of workers died in fires, explosions, floods, and collapses at Pennsylvania mines. One of the worst anthracite mine disasters occurred at Avondale in September 1869, when a fire broke out in the mine, causing the shaft to collapse. One hundred ten workers were killed, including children.

Ninety years later, in 1959, the Knox Mine Disaster served as a death knell to an industry already in decline. An illegal mine shaft built too close to the bed of the Susquehanna River caused the rock

WPA promotional poster, 1937

riverbed to break, creating a 150-foot-wide chasm and sending billions of gallons of river water into connected mine shafts throughout the Wyoming Valley. In all, twelve miners perished (their bodies were never recovered), but thousands more lost their jobs as mining operations shut down.

The coal industry employs about two thousand workers in Pennsylvania today, and the Coal Region still holds about seven billion tons of reserves within its earth. Some coal workers still engage in underground mining, but most work to process the unused coal on slag hills, restoring the hills to their natural beauty.

Three museums and several coal-mine tours allow visitors to explore the history of this important industry. The village of Eckley in Luzerne County was established as a company town, or "patch town," in the 1850s, and today the Eckley Miners' Village preserves the workers' houses, master's house, breaker, churches, and other structures from the mining era. Eckley served as the set for the 1970 film *The Molly Maguires*. It is part of the Anthracite Museum Complex, which also includes the Anthracite Heritage Museum in Scranton, the Scranton Iron Furnaces, and the Museum of Anthracite Mining in Ashland.

Lackawanna coal mine tour, Scranton

THE LABOR MOVEMENT

With the growth of Pennsylvania's mining, lumber, railroad, and other industries in the late nineteenth and early twentieth centuries, organized labor movements emerged seeking fair wages and safer working conditions. While industry leaders such as Henry Clay Frick and Asa Packer amassed great personal fortunes, many workers lived in squalid conditions and labored long hours. Immigrant communities, which made up much of the workforce in the Coal Region, were particularly active in the struggle for workers' rights. Work stoppages and demands for better wages were often met with fierce and, at times, violent resistance from the owners. The Irish Molly Maguires clashed frequently with mining companies on behalf of the miners during this period.

A statue in the courtyard of the Lackawanna County Courthouse in Scranton honors the legendary labor leader John Mitchell (1870–1919). Born into a poor Irish family and orphaned at age six, Mitchell went to work in the mines as a child to help support the family. At the age of fifteen, he joined the Knights of Labor. A founding member of the United Mine Workers of

Sun Village boarding house, Philadelphia

America (UMWA), he served as its president from 1898 to 1907. Mitchell was instrumental in uniting the disparate ethnic groups that were employed at the mines, and during his tenure as union president, UMWA membership increased nearly tenfold. In 1902, Mitchell's UMWA brought the coal industry to a virtual standstill for nine months when about one hundred fifty thousand workers walked off the job in the great Anthracite Coal Strike.

While the Coal Region's mining operations were a hotbed of labor activity, many other industries were active in the labor movement. Urban factory workers, also often subjected to substandard conditions, organized into unions. Workers in the Philadelphia shipping industry lived in cramped quarters, such as the Sun Village boarding house.

Union membership in Pennsylvania has decreased over the years (from twenty-three percent of the workforce in 1989 to less than fourteen percent in 2005), but workers continue to strive for better wages and benefits. In the summer of 2006, service-industry workers, including nurses and social workers, under the Service Employees International Union (SEIU) staged a rally at the capitol in Harrisburg.

Pennsylvania Sugar Company, Philadelphia

*Service Employees International Union
(SEIU) rally, Harrisburg, 2006*

Statue of John Mitchell, Scranton

Scranton panorama, 1912

SCRANTON

Once dominated by the mining, iron, and railroad industries, the Coal Region cities of Scranton and Wilkes-Barre have transformed themselves—following the economic hardships that came with the decline of coal mining in the latter half of the twentieth century—into lively cities that attract students, small businesses, and tourists in the valley just northwest of the popular Pocono Mountains vacation area. With no fewer than ten institutions of higher learning, as well as concert halls and a world-class outdoor amphitheater, the region hosts numerous cultural events. Though independent-minded cities in their own right, Scranton and Wilkes-Barre have collaborated to build an airport and recreational facilities.

Scranton's art museum thrives with programs for school children, a downtown shopping mall attracts shoppers, and the huge Lackawanna Railroad Station has been converted into a five-star hotel. Capitalizing on its industrial and transportation heritage, Scranton is home to the Steamtown National Historic Site, the Electric City Trolley Museum, and the Scranton Iron Furnaces.

Restored lobby and dining room at Lackawanna Railroad Station

Lackawanna Railroad Station, 1930s

Postcard view of Lackawanna County Courthouse

Lackawanna County Courthouse

Above: *Wilkes-Barre aerial*
Below: *Wilkes-Barre panorama, 1909*

WILKES-BARRE

Situated on the banks of the Susquehanna River, Wilkes-Barre bears marks of the past and present. Several of the city's nineteenth-century mansions are occupied by Wilkes University, a school that is a pioneer in developing educational links to China and other nations. The university's modern student center sits on the same street as historic Victorian homes furnished in period style.

Farmers' Market in Public Square

Wilkes-Barre and the Wyoming Valley

Wilkes-Barre was founded in 1769, and it flourished with the discovery of anthracite coal, beginning in the early 1800s. Coal mining drove the city's economy for generations, but as the city closest to the Knox Mine, Wilkes-Barre faced heavy repercussions from the 1959 disaster. The unemployment rate reached twelve percent in the years following the Knox Mine Disaster.

Today, a resurgent Wilkes-Barre is a worthwhile stop for travelers to northeastern Pennsylvania. A farmers' market on the downtown square is a seasonal attraction in summertime, in addition to such year-round attractions as the concert hall, numerous parks, Wilkes University, and shopping.

Above: *Early logging operations*
Right: *Lackawanna Lumber Company logging train*

THE LOGGING INDUSTRY

Pennsylvania's industrial boom of the late 1800s—driven by coal, iron, oil, and the railroads—required hillsides of timber to make charcoal to fuel ironworks and to support a building boom. With little foresight for the future, logging companies stripped mountains bare of trees. The cut logs were transported by train or floated down the Susquehanna, Allegheny, and Delaware Rivers to sawmills, where they were turned into planks for the construction of homes and bridges, for railroad ties, or for the furniture and implement industries.

With the exception of about a dozen preserved native stands of white pine and hemlock, most of Pennsylvania's forests were cut in the nineteenth century. Today, the sixty percent of Pennsylvania that is forest consists of stands of trees that are seventy-five to one hundred years old. "Forest harvesting" proceeds under a state-mandated protocol to maintain forest diversity and prevent clear-cutting. Lumbering has become a relatively minor industry in the state's economy.

In many chief logging towns, such as Williamsport, restaurants and other establishments are sometimes decorated with photos of the glory days of logging, when most households had men employed by the industry. West of Galeton, in sparsely populated Potter County, the Pennsylvania Lumber Museum offers visitors a chance to step back in time and explore the life of a nineteenth-century logger. The museum features a loggers' mess hall, boarding houses, a sawmill, and other replicas of the period, including a Shaw locomotive especially built for logging.

Modern logging truck

LOCK HAVEN

In early America, the towns of Pennsylvania were mere outposts, sometimes fortified against Indian attacks. As the settlements grew, they required a town plan. Lock Haven, in central Pennsylvania, is a classic example of a plan brought to reality. Its streets and center were planned in 1833, and the city thrived with the canal and, later, railroad that linked the businesses to other communities. Covered wooden bridges were built to facilitate crossing the Susquehanna River. As with most Pennsylvania communities, Lock Haven's history is marked by cycles of good times and bad times, influenced by the state's economy, natural disasters, and changes in the fortunes of industry or individual corporations. As the lumber industry declined around the turn of the twentieth century, Lock Haven suffered heavy unemployment for decades.

Above: *Covered bridge across the Susquehanna River at Lock Haven*
Below: *Main Street, Lock Haven, during 1936 flood*

In 1938, Lock Haven received a huge lift when the Piper Corporation, manufacturer of the Piper Cub airplane, opened a factory here. Other companies followed. In 1972, Hurricane Agnes caused major flood damage to the city, and ownership struggles at the Piper Corporation led to the closure of the Lock Haven plant in the mid-1980s, giving the city's residents another shocking down cycle.

The city gradually rebounded, and thanks to grants to renovate historic structures and "Main Street" assistance programs, much of its historic district has been restored. A major flood protection project in the 1990s provided a new levee and floodwall to protect against the ever-present threat of Susquehanna floods. The city, which has about nine thousand year-round residents, is home to the state-funded Lock Haven University of Pennsylvania. The county courthouse stands as erect as ever, although the old covered bridge is gone.

Located in the north-central sector of the state, where the population is thin, this small city has a somewhat isolated economy. Jobs lost during the bad times are not easily absorbed by surrounding communities. Keeping the youth within the community or attracting them back after college becomes a top priority of planners. The city must compete with others across the state for new industries, such as technology companies, to supply higher-paying jobs. Lock Haven is a case study in local economic cycles, but it is not alone, as most Pennsylvania towns are similarly affected.

Above: *Clinton County Court House, Lock Haven*
Left: *Canoeing class on the Susquehanna*

Postcard of Little League World Series

Taiwanese fans at Little League World Series

LITTLE LEAGUE WORLD SERIES

Williamsport has many attractions: paddlewheel boats on the Susquehanna River, a restored historic hotel and restaurant, and the state's premier industrial arts school (the Pennsylvania College of Technology). But every year in August, the city's fame extends around the globe, when teams from Europe, Asia, the Caribbean, and Latin America battle teams from the United States for the world championship of Little League Baseball. Hotels for miles around fill up with families of the players, reporters, and officials. Little League Village, off limits to nearly everyone but the players, is a busy, congenial meeting place.

The Little League World Series was instituted in 1947 with only teams from the United States. The hometown Williamsport club won the inaugural championship, and in 1957, Monterrey, Mexico, became the first international winner. The Far East started dominating the series championships in the late 1960s, and teams from Taiwan brought home the series trophy ten times between 1969 and 1981, including five in a row (1977–1981). California has represented the greatest number of American championship teams. Since 2000, the Little League champions have come from Venezuela, Japan, Curaçao, Hawaii, Kentucky, and Georgia.

Team captains from Japan and the United States shaking hands before game

Above: *Howard J. Lamade Stadium, 2005 Little League World Series*

The Little League World Series has been played at Howard J. Lamade Stadium, in South Williamsport, since the 1950s. When the tournament was expanded from eight teams to sixteen teams in 2001, a second venue, Volunteer Stadium, was opened for the early rounds. Lamade Stadium seats about ten thousand spectators, but as many as thirty thousand more can catch the action from the grassy hill beyond the outfield. Volunteer Stadium accommodates about five thousand.

On Route 15 overlooking the ball park, the Peter J. McGovern Little League Museum is open year-round. At the museum you can learn about the history of Little League Baseball, and kids can pitch and bat against automated opponents. The Hall of Excellence celebrates former Little Leaguers who have gone on to distinguished careers, in baseball and other pursuits.

Army-Navy game, Franklin Field, Philadelphia, 1908

PENNSYLVANIA SPORTS

Pennsylvania is home to seven major league professional sports teams—baseball's Philadelphia Phillies and Pittsburgh Pirates, football's Philadelphia Eagles and Pittsburgh Steelers, hockey's Philadelphia Flyers and Pittsburgh Penguins, and basketball's Philadelphia 76ers—as well as several minor league franchises and many prestigious collegiate programs.

During college football season, millions of fans from throughout the state turn their attention to the city of State College in north-central Pennsylvania, home of the Penn State University Nittany Lions. The team's coach, Joe Paterno, is a true Pennsylvania icon. "Joe Pa" first joined the Penn State coaching staff in 1950, and since becoming head coach in 1966, he has led the Lions to more than 360 wins and two national championships (as of 2006).

On home game dates, all roads to Penn State's Beaver Stadium are bumper to bumper with cars heading to Happy Valley. The stadium seats 107,283, which is about three times the population of State College. The tailgate parties and campouts are half the fun for many Nittany Lions fans.

In the professional ranks, the NFL's Eagles and Steelers battle for the attention and loyalty of Pennsylvania's pigskin fans. When the cities of Philadelphia and Pittsburgh were looking to replace their multipurpose, cookie-cutter stadiums in the early 2000s—Veterans Stadium in Philly and Three Rivers Stadiums in Pittsburgh—both opted to build separate homes for their baseball and football teams. In Philadelphia, the $512-million Lincoln Financial Field was inaugurated with a soccer match between European giants Manchester United and FC Barcelona in August

Beaver Stadium broadcast booth, Penn State, 1951

Statue outside Lincoln Financial Field, Philadelphia

Beaver Stadium, Penn State

Pittsburgh Steelers game at Three Rivers Stadium, 1990s

Heinz Field exterior, Pittsburgh

2003. The Eagles played their first game in the new 68,500-seat stadium a month later.

Since 2003, the annual Army-Navy game has been played at Lincoln Financial Field. This long-standing college football tradition has been played in Philadelphia more often than any other city, first at the University of Pennsylvania's Franklin Field (on and off between 1899 and 1935) before moving on to Municipal Stadium (later known as John F. Kennedy Stadium) and then Veterans Stadium.

Heinz Field, home of the Pittsburgh Steelers, opened in 2001. It debuted in the same year as its baseball neighbor, PNC Park, along the banks of the Allegheny River. From the South Plaza, Heinz Field offers a view of Point State Park and the downtown skyline. The football arena seats 64,450, and it also serves as the home field for the University of Pittsburgh Panthers.

The history of baseball in Philadelphia and Pittsburgh dates back to the 1800s, and the cities have experienced highs, and some very low lows, on the diamond. The Phillies and Pirates have also played in some of the game's most celebrated ballparks, including the palatial Shibe Park (later Connie Mack Stadium) and Forbes Field. After a thirty-year tenure at the rather unglamorous Veterans Stadium and Three Rivers Stadium, the cities of Philadelphia and Pittsburgh have invested in new, state-of-the-art baseball facilities, both of which were designed to fit within the architecture and layout of their urban neighborhoods. Both parks also incorporate sculptures, murals, and other artwork honoring the local history of our national pastime.

Opened in 2004, Philadelphia's Citizens Bank Park cost nearly $350 million to build (compared to Shibe Park's $450,000 price tag in 1909), with financing split almost evenly between private and public funding sources. It is part of a massive sports complex in South Philly that also includes the Eagles' Lincoln Financial Field; the Wachovia Center, home to the Flyers and 76ers; and the Wachovia Spectrum, the oldest of the complex's arenas and now used for a variety of events. Among its distinctive features, Citizens Bank Park includes a rooftop bleacher section—harking

"Ashburn Alley" concessions concourse, Citizens Bank Park

Above: *Forbes Field entrance, Pittsburgh, 1909*
Below: *1910 World Series, Shibe Park, Philadelphia*

back to the "wildcat" rooftop seating that was built by fans who lived across the street from the old Shibe Park. A fifty-foot-tall, neon re-creation of the Liberty Bell rings out in celebration of every Phillies home run.

Though it is the league's smallest ballpark, PNC Park in Pittsburgh opened in 2001 with a host of amenities, including a view of the city skyline across the Allegheny River. Fans arrive at the park by car, foot, or riverboat; the Roberto Clemente Bridge, which provides access to the stadium's North Side location from downtown, is closed to automotive traffic on game days. Like its Philadelphia equivalent, PNC Park evokes the city's baseball past in its architecture and features, as well as providing a family-friendly atmosphere.

Citizens Bank Park, Philadelphia, 2007

PNC Park, Pittsburgh, 2007

SCENIC HIGHWAYS

Pennsylvania's highway system offers a pleasant and convenient way to escape the urban and suburban sprawl and venture into the state's vast countryside and wilderness. The Pennsylvania Turnpike, known as "America's First Super Highway," had its origins in 1884, long before the advent of the automobile, when William H. Vanderbilt built a roadbed and dug tunnels through the Allegheny ridges for his planned South Pennsylvania Railroad. The project stalled, however, and several of the proposed nine tunnels filled with water.

By the 1930s and 1940s, the vision for a high-speed super highway began to take shape. No hills, no cross streets—just smooth, fast riding for motorists cruising across Pennsylvania.

More than one thousand engineers were hired to finish the tunnel designs and outline the unprecedented four-lane, divided roadway, featuring a two-hundred-foot right of way. Devised for fast driving, the roadway's curves would have a maximum bend of six degrees, and the maximum grade would be just three percent. Compared with the hilly Lincoln Highway—the nation's first transcontinental roadway—the Pennsylvania Turnpike was groundbreaking.

At the opening on October 1, 1940, a Sunday, more automobiles came to try out the turnpike than could be managed. Cars were lined up for miles to pay tolls and exit. Still, many motorists were able to take advantage of the highway's revolutionary design; one driver reported averaging ninety-one miles per hour on his drive. Most cars ignored the governor's fifty-mile-per-hour limit, which had been announced just before the opening.

While the turnpike and subsequent interstates like I-80 and I-81 provide fine panoramic scenery of forests and farmlands, many winding, two-lane roads across the state have been improved in recent decades and continue to offer an intimate and scenic driving experience—at a slower pace. Route 6, across the northern tier of the state, is especially picturesque, as is Route 120 in Clinton and Cameron counties, particularly in autumn when the foliage radiates in brilliant shades of red, orange, and yellow.

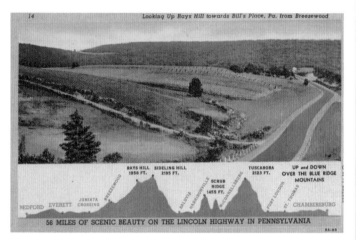

Postcard view of Rays Hill along Lincoln Highway

U.S. Route 322 along the Juniata River

Intersection of I-81, Route 22, and Route 322, near Harrisburg

Above: *Blue Mountain tunnel on the Pennsylvania Turnpike, Franklin County*

Aerial of Pennsylvania Turnpike, Bedford County

Below: *Fall color along Route 6, Potter County*

Vacation cabins, state park

Family picnic, state park

Swimming at Powder Hole Falls, Luzerne County

Primitive cabins in Black Moshannon State Park, Centre County

Family picnic, state park

Kayaking on the Youghiogheny River, Ohiopyle State Park, Fayette County

Camping at Worlds End State Park, Sullivan County

STATE PARKS AND FORESTS

A state park within twenty-five miles of every Pennsylvanian"—that was the vision of Dr. Maurice Goddard. In the 1950s, Goddard picked up the crusade of Gifford Pinchot, the great conservationist of the early 1900s. Pinchot, who was the first head of the federal government's Division of Forestry (later the U.S. Forest Service) and a two-term governor of Pennsylvania, advocated the management and protection of public lands, a position that Goddard pursued while he served as Secretary of the Pennsylvania Department of Forests and Waters.

Under Pinchot and Goddard's leadership, Pennsylvania established one of the nation's largest parks systems. With 128 state parks and 18 state forests covering 2.4 million acres, all Pennsylvanians have easy access to state lands for hiking, camping, swimming, kayaking, and other outdoor activities. Endless miles of protected creeks and rivers, trails, and forestland provide respite and recreation for visitors and residents alike. Parks range from remote and little-trod to more popular parks with a full range of cabin accommodations, lakes, nature centers, and camper hookups. In the expansive state forests, one can drive on primitive roads or hike for tens of miles surrounded by nothing but the sounds and beauty of the pristine wilderness.

FISHING

According to the Pennsylvania Campaign for Clean Water, the state has 83,184 miles of rivers and streams and 161,445 acres of ponds and lakes—plenty of places to fish for trout and bass. Fishing provides forty-seven thousand jobs and brings in $4.7 billion in revenue to the state each year.

Some of Pennsylvania's trout streams, such as the Yellow Breeches Creek in central Pennsylvania, are among the best in the northeastern United States. Trout season opens in April, when streams close to population centers are well stocked with fish and lined with eager fishermen. The more adventuresome fly fishermen will drive or hike into remote areas for the solitude they desire.

Ice fishing is a sport practiced by a few committed Pennsylvanians, although an abundance of frozen lakes in the winter offer plenty of opportunity.

Ice fishing on Lake Erie

Trout fisherman, Dauphin County

Fly fishing on Boiling Springs, Cumberland County

Ice fishing in Hills Creek State Park, Tioga County

SKIING

The ski resorts of the Pocono Mountains and in the Laurel Highlands of southwestern Pennsylvania—such as Big Boulder, Camelback, Hidden Valley, and Seven Springs—offer a range of challenging downhill slopes and first-class lodges. Many other ski slopes and lodges dot Pennsylvania's mountain areas, catering to all levels of skiers and snowboarders. In the early twentieth century, advertisements and brochures featuring models posed in ski gear lured people out to the slopes. The historic photos show that skiing was a popular activity at a time when a primary means of travel was train rather than automobile.

Above: *Skiing in the Poconos*
Right: *Skiing at Ski Roundtop, Lewisberry*

HORSEBACK RIDING AND HORSE RACING

In eastern and central Pennsylvania, horse farms and riding clubs abound. The town of Devon in Chester County, in the heart of horse country, holds a popular and challenging performance competition every year. For others, horseback riding is an appealing diversion for leisure or just to get away. The hilly terrain of York, Cumberland, and Chester counties offers a variety of settings for scenic rides, including high lookout areas. Occasionally, one finds horseback riders on the Appalachian Trail.

For horse lovers of a different bent, Pennsylvania is home to five horse racing venues, including Penn National Race Course at

Horseback riding, state park

Horse jumping, Chester County

Grantville, in central Pennsylvania. On race days, the course is a beehive of activity as spectators cheer on their favorite thoroughbreds, hoping to cash in on a big winner. The Meadows, outside of Pittsburgh, offers harness racing year-round. Beginning in 2005, new venues have opened where people can bet on horse races, including Philadelphia Park Casino and Racetrack, Harrah's Chester Downs, Presque Isle Downs in Erie, and Mohegan Sun at Pocono Downs.

Horseback riding in William H. Kain County Park, York County

Penn National Race Course, Grantville

Cathedral of the Most Blessed Sacrament

ALTOONA

Strategically located at the foot of the Allegheny Mountains, the city of Altoona was founded in the mid-nineteenth century by the Pennsylvania Railroad (PRR), which built its locomotive construction facility and maintenance shops here. The city was situated where the main PRR line began its arduous climb over and tunneling through the mountains on the westward runs to Pittsburgh. Altoona became a vital hub in the PRR's vast network. The company employed as many as fifteen thousand Altoona residents at its peak in the 1920s. By the end of World War II, Altoona was the world's largest railroad repair and manufacturing complex.

Although the days of the railroad boom have long since past, freight traffic still passes through the mountain tunnels here, with the tunnel heights raised to accommodate cars carrying two truck trailers stacked together. Amtrak also passes through Altoona on its daily run between New York City and Chicago.

Postcard view of Altoona and Pennsylvania Railroad shops

Now a city of about fifty thousand residents, Altoona's skyline is marked by the dome of the Cathedral of the Most Blessed Sacrament, which was constructed between 1924 and 1960.

Horseshoe Curve, 1934

HORSESHOE CURVE

Since February 1854, train riders and spectators alike have marveled at the 2,375-foot curvature of the railroad a few miles west of Altoona as it climbs the first range of the Allegheny Mountains. Built by the Pennsylvania Railroad, Horseshoe Curve is on a 220-degree arc on two curves. The west side of the curve is 122 feet higher than the east side as the tracks make their way up the mountains.

Named a National Historic Landmark in 1966, Horseshoe Curve has a museum and locomotive display for visitors who drive to the site. Steps lead to the railroad tracks, where one can watch trains make the turn every twenty minutes.

Horseshoe Curve

East Broad Top steam locomotive, Orbisonia

RAILROADS IN PENNSYLVANIA

Across the state—from Altoona to Scranton, Strasburg to Hummelstown—the impact of the railroads on Pennsylvania communities can be experienced firsthand. Several museums honor the contributions made by railroads and railroaders to American industry and progress, and heritage railways and restored railcars allow visitors, young and old alike, to relive the days when trains carried people and cargo to all corners of the state and beyond.

The dominant player in railroads for more than a century was the Pennsylvania Railroad. Founded in 1846, the PRR was originally chartered to connect Philadelphia and Pittsburgh by way of Harrisburg, but its scope quickly expanded. By the 1880s, the PRR increased its network by acquiring lines to Baltimore, Washington, New York, and New Jersey to the east, and to Cleveland, Indianapolis, Chicago, St. Louis, and other points west. The PRR set the standard for railroad engineering and innovation worldwide. It initiated consistent design, which created greater efficiency in railcar and locomotive manufacturing.

Altoona locomotive repair shop, circa 1903

Pennsylvania Railroad, West Philadelphia, circa 1874

Tourist excursion through Lackawanna County, Steamtown National Historic Site

Excursion on the historic Gettysburg Express, *Adams County*

The PRR's Altoona shops, along with the Baldwin Locomotive Works in the Philadelphia area, were the leading builders of steam, electric, and diesel locomotives.

In 1968, the PRR merged with its chief competitor, the New York Central, to form Penn Central, which went bankrupt two years later. The Penn Central's lines were split between Amtrak and Conrail. Today, most of Conrail's old PRR lines are operated by the Norfolk Southern Railway.

Altoona's Railroaders Memorial Museum, housed in the PRR's 1882 Master Mechanics Building, pays homage to the area's railroading heritage. At the Steamtown National Historic Site in Scranton, numerous exhibits and displays—including restored rail cars, an old roundhouse, and the Locomotive Repair Shop—tell the

story of steam railroading. The *Scranton Limited*, powered by either steam or diesel locomotive, carries visitors on old-style tours through the surrounding countryside.

The East Broad Top Railroad, based in Rockville Furnace, was a narrow-gauge railway that transported coal, ore, and other products in south-central Pennsylvania beginning in 1873. After the EBT ceased operation in 1956, the complete railroad was preserved as a tourist site, including the locomotives, rolling stock, shops, and other buildings. Today, the East Broad Top Railroad operates steam-powered excursions along the original narrow-gauge tracks.

At Strasburg, the Railroad Museum of Pennsylvania includes exhibits of railroad history, and the nearby Strasburg Rail Road offers excursions through Lancaster County farmland.

View near Main Street after the flood, 1889

Flood damage, 1889

View of Johnstown after the flood, 1889

THE JOHNSTOWN FLOOD

Floods caused by heavy rains that fill mountain streams, which rush into the Lehigh, Delaware, Allegheny, or Susquehanna River valleys, are not unusual, despite many flood-control dams and dikes. Two hundred thousand residents were evacuated from Wilkes-Barre in 2006 as a precautionary measure, in case the waters of the Susquehanna breeched the dike. Fortunately, the river stopped short of the dike's ridge at Wilkes-Barre, but in other towns, the water rose to window levels and higher. More than thirty years earlier, Wilkes-Barre had suffered major damage from flooding caused by Hurricane Agnes, resulting in an estimated $1 billion in damage.

Although floods have left their mark on Pennsylvania towns and countryside for centuries, the Johnstown Flood of 1889 was unique in its devastation. In the late 1870s, the South Fork Fishing and Hunting Club rebuilt the old South Fork Dam on the Conemaugh River to create a lakeside resort for the wealthy of Pittsburgh. The club's dam proved to be faulty, however, and on May 31, 1889, in a record downpour, the dam burst. A mighty pillar of water sixty feet high came pouring down the valley at speeds of forty miles per hour toward the city of Johnstown, which had a population of about thirty thousand at the time. The power and force of the water carried locomotives with it and pummeled the city with little warning. In a matter of minutes, homes were smashed, lives were lost, and much of the city was carried into the flatland downriver. Johnstown lay in ruins. About twenty-two hundred were left dead, including ninety-nine entire

View from atop the Johnstown Inclined Plane

Johnstown Flood National Memorial

families. The Grandview Cemetery holds the Plot of the Unknown, where are buried more than 750 bodies that were never identified. It took years to clean up the devastation.

Johnstown has been hit by other major floods—most recently, a July 1977 deluge that left much of the city under several feet of water—but none was as destructive as the Great Flood of 1889.

Today, you can learn about the details of the Great Flood at the Johnstown Heritage Museum and the Johnstown Flood Museum, which includes a theater where a movie tells the dramatic story of the club, the dam, and the disaster. The Johnstown Flood National Memorial is located near the site of the South Fork Fishing and Hunting Club and includes the remains of the old dam.

In Johnstown, a ride on the incline car, which residents living on the hilltop take to and from the city center, brings you to a platform at the top of the incline, from where you can look out over the rebuilt city and imagine the events of the terrible flood.

FORT NECESSITY

In southwestern Pennsylvania, along U.S. Highway 40, is the site of an English fort where the opening battle of the French and Indian War took place in the summer of 1754. The war, which was part of the global Seven Years' War between France and England, would determine which colonial power gained control of America.

With French forces secured in their position at the fork of the Ohio River (now Pittsburgh), George Washington, then a lieutenant colonel in the British army, led a Virginia regiment to encamp in a marshy meadow to the south. Here they built a small fort, which became known as Fort Necessity, in anticipation of battle with the French and their Native American allies. After the English scored a decisive victory in a surprise attack on a smaller French regiment at Jumonville Glen nearby, the French arrived in full force at the British encampment. The ensuing battle took the lives of many on both sides, with Washington's forces suffering the greatest loss. A truce was reached, and the French allowed Washington's forces to retreat. This was the first and last defeat for Washington in his military career.

Fort Necessity National Battlefield

Log house at Fort Necessity National Battlefield

Fort Necessity was burned by the French following the battle, but nearly two centuries later, the site was preserved as a National Battlefield Site. The fort was first reconstructed in a triangular configuration in the 1930s, but subsequent archeological research revealed that the original structure was in fact circular. Fort Necessity was rebuilt in a circular configuration in the 1950s.

The visitors' center at Fort Necessity National Battlefield includes maps and graphic explanations of the French and Indian War. You can explore the fort, take a trail to Jumonville Glen, or visit the burial place of General Edward Braddock.

Mount Washington Tavern, formerly the Fort Necessity Museum

Mount Washington Tavern

MOUNT WASHINGTON TAVERN
AND THE NATIONAL ROAD

When U.S. Highway 40, originally known as the National Road, was first built during the early 1800s, it was the first highway constructed exclusively with funding from the federal government. Beginning at Cumberland, Maryland, the National Road cut through the southwest corner of Pennsylvania on its way to Vandalia, Illinois, where construction ended due to lack of funds. Towns and travelers' rest stops flourished along the route, among them the Mount Washington Tavern, built in the 1820s near Uniontown.

Although activity on the National Road declined dramatically during the railroad era, the road experienced a revival during the early years of automobile travel in the twentieth century. Highway 40, established in the 1920s, followed closely the original road's alignment in Pennsylvania.

The Mount Washington Tavern has been restored with period furnishings and is open to visitors. It consists of a barroom, parlor, dining room, kitchen, and bedrooms.

Period kitchen display, Mount Washington Tavern

Allegheny Reservoir and Allegheny National Forest

ALLEGHENY NATIONAL FOREST

Located within a day's drive of one-third of the nation's population, the vast Allegheny National Forest consists of 510,000 acres spread through the wilds of McKean, Warren, Elk, and Forest counties in northwestern Pennsylvania. The Allegheny River—which originates in Potter County to the east before looping through New York and zigzagging south toward its convergence with the Monongahela River in Pittsburgh—flows through the western boundary of the national forest. The Kinzua Dam, built in the 1960s near Warren, formed the Allegheny Reservoir in the northwest corner of the national forest.

By the time the Allegheny National Forest was established in 1923, much of the area had been clear-cut by loggers during the industrial boom of the late 1800s and early 1900s. The wildlife population, particularly deer, also had been largely depleted. With the creation of the national forest, the lands were replanted with maples, birches, cherries, and other tree species, and wildlife gradually returned.

Although most of the forest today is second-growth, a virgin stand of white pine and hemlock, two hundred to three hundred years old, can be seen at Heart's Content. The area is a favorite spot for strolls under the heavy canopy of pine needles, or as a quiet sanctuary for meditation or contemplation.

Hundreds of miles of trails wind through the Allegheny National Forest, leading to many scenic overlooks, and the forest's sixteen campgrounds contain more than six hundred campsites. The Allegheny Reservoir offers over one hundred miles of shoreline and ample recreational activities.

Heavily logged forest in Tioga County, circa 1920

Old-growth forest at Heart's Content

Right: *Octave Oil Company wells near Titusville, 1882*
Below: *Workers at oil wells*

OIL IN THE KEYSTONE STATE

Native Americans were the first to discover oil flowing from "oil springs" in what today is Pennsylvania, and they used it in ceremonies and for medicinal uses long before the arrival of Europeans. In 1850, Samuel Kier began refining the crude oil, and he packaged it as a medicinal product called "Seneca Oil." He later found an economical way to refine the oil into kerosene for use in lamps.

Hoping to build on Kier's work with refined oil, Edwin Drake and William "Uncle Billy" Smith started drilling for large quantities of crude in northwestern Pennsylvania. On August 27, 1889, the men struck oil, at a depth of sixty-nine-and-a-half feet, along Oil Creek near Titusville, in Venango County—and the American petroleum industry was born. Over the next ten years, 5,500 wells were drilled in the area, of which 1,186 produced oil. By 1861, 2.5 million barrels of crude oil were taken from the ground.

Today, the Drake Oil Museum, located near Oil City, tells the story of the oil boom and the boom towns that supported the drilling operations during the nineteenth century. The museum contains a replica of the first oil well.

Replica of Edwin Drake's oil well, Drake Oil Museum

Postcard view of Erie docks, 1916

ERIE AND GREAT LAKES SHIPPING

Erie, today the fourth-largest city in Pennsylvania, was first settled by the French in the 1750s. After coming under British rule following the French and Indian War, the city of Erie was claimed by several colonies. It officially became part of Pennsylvania in 1792, providing the state with a Great Lakes port.

During the War of 1812, Commodore Oliver Perry was sent to Erie in 1813 to oversee the construction of a small fleet. At the time, the city had only five hundred residents, and laborers as well as materials had to be transported to Erie from Pittsburgh, Philadelphia, and other cities. By midsummer, six vessels were completed, including the brigs *Niagara* and *Lawrence*. In September, Perry's fleet sailed into battle on Lake Erie, where they defeated a British squadron in the dramatic Battle of Lake Erie. The victory helped to lift American morale, established a safe passage for supplies, and secured the Northwest Territories.

Postcard view of fishing boat in Erie harbor

The *Niagara* was reconstructed to historic detail in the late 1980s, and it is now part of the Erie Maritime Museum, administered by the Pennsylvania Historical and Museum Commission. Visitors can explore the ship in its berth, and during the summer, the *Niagara* sets sail from Erie harbor. The museum features additional exhibits and interactive displays to illustrate the maritime heritage along this forty-mile stretch of Lake Erie.

The docks of the city's harbor are filled with leisure and fishing boats that ply the waters of the lake. Erie is also the gateway to Presque Isle State Park, located on a slender peninsula that juts into the lake. The park provides fine bird watching, swimming, biking, or hiking opportunities.

Erie's revitalized downtown features a variety of shops and restaurants, as well as two large city parks, one of which has a farmers' market and the other a gazebo for evening entertainment. Additional downtown attractions include the Erie Art Museum, at Discovery Square; the historic 1927 Ford Hotel, which was remodeled into the Richford Arms apartments in the late 1970s; and the neoclassical courthouse. The double-A Erie Seawolves baseball team has a downtown ballpark, and the Civic Center is home to the Erie Otters ice hockey.

Above: *Boat launch at Erie harbor*
Right: *Reconstructed brig* Niagara *at the Erie Maritime Museum*

Pittsburgh skyline, 1904

PITTSBURGH

Situated at the confluence of three rivers, the site of the city of Pittsburgh was a strategic battleground in the colonial struggle for supremacy in America. The French first established Fort Duquesne here, in 1754. The British subsequently built a new fortification called Fort Pitt, after William Pitt, then Secretary of State and later Prime Minister of England.

Pittsburgh grew as an industrial center throughout the nineteenth century, with such innovative businessmen such as Andrew Carnegie, Henry Clay Frick, Henry J. Heinz, Andrew W. Mellon, and George Westinghouse. A booming steel industry earned it the nickname "Steel City," and by 1910, Pittsburgh had more than half a million residents and was the eighth-largest city in the United States.

In the years following World War II, a citywide renaissance program sought to transform the city from one of dense smog and industrial pollution to a clean city representing progress. The decline of the steel industry in the 1970s and 1980s, however, led to hard times, high unemployment, and a population decline. A second Renaissance has been underway since the 1990s, with an emphasis on developing the high-tech, medical, and service industries. Where U.S. Steel once employed tens of thousands of residents, the University of Pittsburgh Medical Center is today the city's largest employer. Through the city's two renaissance periods, Mellon Bank, Pittsburgh Paint and Glass (PPG), U.S. Steel, and other corporations have invested billions of dollars in gleaming downtown office buildings—some of the most stylish in the country— as well as contributing to the city's general welfare.

Pittsburgh skyline, 1920

Left: Pittsburgh skyline

Postcard view of Pittsburgh skyline, 1940s

THE POINT

The most vivid exposure of Pittsburgh's past and present can be seen at the Point, the V-shaped piece of land where the Allegheny and Monongahela rivers meet to form the Ohio River. During the earliest European exploration of and settlement in the region, the Point was the location of Fort Duquesne and Fort Pitt, the major fortification and defense of the gateway to the West.

In the industrial era, when Pittsburgh steel smelting served the world, the "Point" was a busy but grimy industrial slum—in stark contrast to the Point's revitalized, park-like appearance today. A National Historic Landmark, the thirty-six-acre Point State Park is the apex of Pittsburgh's Golden Triangle. A water fountain, which shoots water 150 feet into the air at a rate of 6,000 gallons per minute, creates a grand spectacle, especially when viewed at night from Mount Washington across the Monongahela. Walking and bicycling trails surround the park's grassy areas, and the park hosts events such as hot-air balloon races, the Three Rivers Regatta, the Three Rivers Arts Festival, and Fourth of July fireworks. The Fort Pitt Museum and the Fort

Pitt Blockhouse (the only remnant of the original fort), as well as numerous plaques and monuments, allow visitors to explore the area's historical significance.

Above: *The Point and downtown Pittsburgh, 1902*

Below: *The Point and downtown Pittsburgh, 2007*

The Point and downtown Pittsburgh, circa 1938

Above: *The Point, viewed from Mount Washington, 1950*
Left: *Aerial view of the Point and the Golden Triangle*

Duquesne and Monongahela Inclines

Early in the twentieth century, more than a dozen inclines operated in Pittsburgh, transporting both industrial materials and commuters up and down the city's steep hillsides. The Penn Incline (also known as the 17th Street Incline) carried coal freight cars between Pittsburgh's Hill and Strip Districts from 1883 until it ceased operation in 1953.

Today, only the Duquesne and Monongahela inclines remain, serving tourists and workers traveling to and from residences, businesses, and restaurants on Mount Washington. From the top, spectacular views emerge of the city skyline, the three rivers, and other Pittsburgh landmarks. In 2003, *USA Weekend Magazine* rated the view from atop Mount Washington as the second most impressive in the nation.

The Duquesne Incline, which opened in 1877, has a new viewing platform from where the cable mechanisms can be seen as well as the cityscape. The incline is operated by the Society for the Preservation of the Duquesne Heights Incline and receives no public funding.

Farther east on Mount Washington, the Monongahela Incline provides a different view of the city and overlooks the southern end of the Smithfield Bridge. The scene is no less spectacular. Built in 1870, the Monongahela Incline has a seventy-eight percent grade.

Penn Incline, 1940s

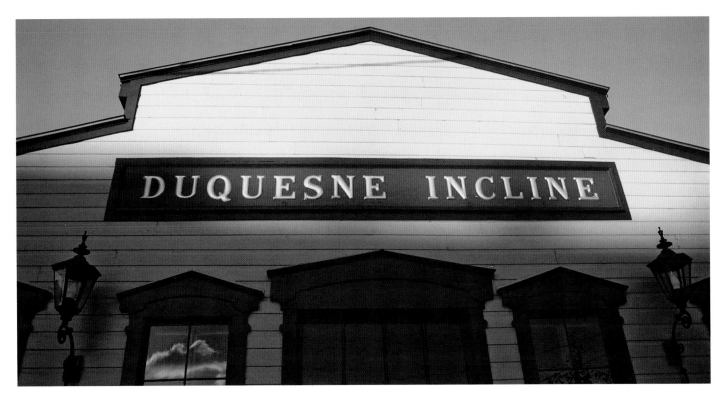

Entrance to Duquesne Incline

Duquesne Incline

Inclined railway to Mount Washington, circa 1907

PITTSBURGH'S BRIDGES

With downtown bounded by rivers on the north and south, and the Ohio River cutting through the city's western end, planners and engineers have had to work overtime to accommodate the flow of traffic through the city. Pittsburgh reportedly has more bridges than any city in the world, and it is commonly referred to as the "City of Bridges." The view from Mount Washington (on a clear day) reveals as many as nineteen bridges dotting the landscape.

Pittsburgh's bridges come in many shapes, sizes, and colors—from sweeping arches to boxy structures, and from rusted steel railroad bridges to the triplet of yellow suspension bridges across the Allegheny River from downtown. The first bridges serving downtown were constructed at Sixth Street, running to the North Side across the Allegheny River, and at Smithfield Street, crossing the Monongahela to the south. The current Smithfield Street Bridge, built in the 1880s, is the oldest river bridge in all of Allegheny County. It links downtown to the South Side. Upstream, the 1,200-foot-long South Tenth Street Bridge is the longest span on the Monongahela.

Along with the Andy Warhol (Seventh Street) Bridge and Rachel Carson (Ninth Street) Bridge, the Roberto Clemente Bridge (formerly the Sixth Street Bridge) is one of the "Three Sisters" that were built between 1924 and 1928 to link downtown with the city's North Side. The bridge was renamed in honor of the former baseball great to coincide with the opening of new Pirates ballpark, PNC Park. It is closed to vehicular traffic on game days, as well as when the Steelers are playing at Heinz Field next door.

View of Monongahela River bridges from Mount Washington

Smithfield Street Bridge

Sixth Street Bridge

Roberto Clemente (Sixth Street) Bridge

SMITHFIELD STREET

Located in the Golden Triangle, Smithfield Street is one of the city's busiest streets. It runs through the heart of downtown and onto the Smithfield Street Bridge, crossing the Monongahela River to Station Square's restaurants and shops and the South Side.

History marches along Smithfield Street, and the historic flavor remains as the buildings change their names but not their architecture. The classical columns of the Mellon Bank building stand as monuments to a time gone by, when residents traveled by trolley or horse-drawn carriage.

Above: *Postcard view of Smithfield Street, late 1800s*
Right: *Smithfield Street, looking north*

TROLLEYS

Pittsburgh's first trolleys hit the streets in the 1890s, and by 1902, the Pittsburgh Railways Company had more than one thousand trolleys operating throughout the city, carrying tens of millions of passengers. As cars and buses became more and more prevalent, the trolleys were pushed aside.

Fortunately, an appreciation for trolleys encouraged the preservation and celebration of this mode of transportation. In the town of Washington, south of Pittsburgh, a group of concerned trolley buffs began collecting old trolleys in the years following World War II, and in 1953, they purchased two thousand feet of abandoned track. The Pennsylvania Trolley Museum in Washington opened to the public in 1963. Today, the museum holds forty-five trolleys in its collection. Visitors can learn about the history of trolleys and streetcars, or take a short ride on a vintage trolley.

Several companies also offer tours of Pittsburgh on buses modified to look like vintage trolleys to recapture the nostalgia of the urban streetcar experience.

Above, top: *Trolley and horse-drawn carriages on Fifth Avenue, 1903*
Above: *Citizens Traction Company cable car on Fifth Avenue, 1890s*

Tourist wheeled trolley

THE CARNEGIE MUSEUMS

In addition to his influence as a pioneering industrialist, Andrew Carnegie was also a dedicated philanthropist, and part of his legacy is a diverse family of museums in the Pittsburgh area. The Carnegie Museums of Pittsburgh is the city's largest arts and culture organization, consisting of four separate and distinct exhibition venues: the Carnegie Museum of Art, the Carnegie Museum of Natural History, the Carnegie Science Center, and the Andy Warhol Museum.

Carnegie opened the Carnegie Museum of Art in 1895 to showcase contemporary art from around the world, and he hosted the first Carnegie International exhibition, now the oldest international exhibition of contemporary art in North America.

Above: *Scaife Galleries, Carnegie Museum of Art*
Below: *Dinosaur Hall, Carnegie Museum of Natural History, 1951*

The Carnegie Museum of Natural History's Dinosaur Hall features a world-renowned collection of dinosaur bones. The most recent addition to the Carnegie Museums family is the Andy Warhol Museum, which opened in 1994. It is one of the largest museums in the world dedicated to a single artist.

HEINZ HALL

L ocated in the heart of downtown's cultural district, Heinz Hall originated as the Loew's Penn Theater, a grand cinema that opened in 1927. After the movie house closed in 1964, the building underwent a massive renovation to become the new home for the Pittsburgh Symphony Orchestra. Dedicated in 1971, Heinz Hall features beautiful reception halls and a 2,661-seat concert hall, all of which were extensively refurbished in 1995. In addition to the Pittsburgh Symphony Orchestra, the internationally renowned hall hosts performances by the Pittsburgh Youth Symphony as well as many national touring acts.

Above: *Crowds outside Heinz Hall, 1960s*
Right: *Heinz Hall interior*

Above: *University of Pittsburgh campus, including Pitt Stadium and the Cathedral of Learning*
Right: *Cathedral of Learning, University of Pittsburgh*
Photo by Theodor Horydczak

Cathedral of Learning, University of Pittsburgh, from Phipps Conservatory

Syrian room in the Cathedral of Learning

UNIVERSITY OF PITTSBURGH

Founded in 1787 in the state's western frontier, the University of Pittsburgh is one of the oldest universities in the country, and the oldest west of the Allegheny Mountains. The campus's most outstanding architectural and historic building is the Cathedral of Learning. At forty-two stories and 535 feet high, the cathedral is the tallest educational building in the Western Hemisphere, and second only to the main tower of Moscow State University worldwide. The interior rooms are furnished and designed according to the culture and style of various nations.

Pitt's urban campus is located in the Oakland section of the city, near Carnegie Mellon University and the Carnegie Museum of Art as well as Schenley Park and the Phipps Conservatory. As a state institution, the University of Pittsburgh offers academic programs at a lower cost than private colleges and universities in the state. Among its many academic programs and graduate studies, the School of Medicine and the University of Pittsburgh Medical Center (UPMC) are leading medical teaching centers and healthcare providers. UPMC operates several hospitals in the Pittsburgh area. The medical research lab became renowned when Jonas Salk invented the polio vaccine there.

INDEX

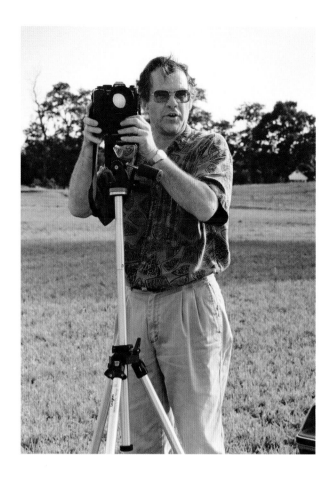

ABOUT THE AUTHOR

Blair Seitz was born in York County, Pennsylvania, and has spent most of his life as a resident of the Keystone State. He began his career as a photojournalist traveling extensively in Africa and Asia on various assignments. In the course of his travels, he visited twenty-one countries, many in midst of political and social turmoil. His essays and photos were widely published in newspapers and magazines, such as the *New York Times Magazine*, *Time*, *Newsweek*, the *Christian Science Monitor,* the *Guardian*, the *South China Morning Post*, *Pacific Magazine*, *New Internationalist*, *Topic*, and *New World Outlook*.

Through agencies in New York, London, and Tokyo as well as BlairSeitz.com, his photographs continue to be published worldwide. Seitz's prints have been exhibited by the World Exhibition of Photography, the Museum of Natural History in New York, and numerous smaller galleries.

Seitz is the photographer of more than twenty books, including *Philadelphia and Its Countryside*, *Pennsylvania Tapestry: Views from the Air*, *Pennsylvania's Natural Beauty*, *Gardens of Philadelphia*, and *Amish Ways*. He currently lives in Wallingford in Chester County.